Building a Career in
COMPLIANCE AND ETHICS

Find your place in the business world's hottest new field

By Joseph E. Murphy and Joshua H. Leet

ISBN 978-0-9792210-0-2

This publication is designed to provide accurate and authoritative information in regard to the subject matter covered. It is sold with the understanding that neither the authors nor the publisher are engaged in rendering legal, accounting, or other professional service. If legal advice or other expert assistance is required, the services of a competent professional person should be sought (from a Declaration of Principles jointly adopted by a Committee of the American Bar Association and a Committee of Publishers).

To order copies of this publication, please contact:

Society of Corporate Compliance & Ethics
6500 Barrie Road, Suite 250
Minneapolis, MN 55435, United States

Phone: +1 952 933 4977
Fax: 952 988 0146
Web site: www.corporatecompliance.org
e-mail: info@corporatecompliance.org

To contact authors Joseph E. Murphy and Joshua H. Leet,
e-mail jemurphy@cslg.com or jleet@cslg.com

Contents

Preface

Corporate fraud. Unsafe products. CEOs sentenced to jail. What can be done to prevent business crimes? Something more than threats from the outside is needed. For corporate professionals engaged in misconduct, the *possibility* that someday, somehow, someone on the "outside" will discover what they are doing and impose punishment seems remote. For some, short-term fears (investors will sell the stock, my boss will be angry with me) will trump a longer-term fear (someday the government might find out what I am doing). If we rely strictly on the legal system, we'll forever be in a catch-up mode: law enforcement takes action only *after* the harm is done.

Is there a better answer? Yes. We can empower people within business to prevent and detect misconduct. But how can business managers, who see their jobs as making money for their shareholders, be expected to undertake this self-policing role? The answer to that question is what the field of corporate compliance and ethics is about.

This field exists to prevent harm at its source and to make powerful organizations safer and more ethical. Many people may expect their government can protect them from the harm corporations and large organizations can cause. But it is the nature of government and the legal system to always be reactive. Compliance and ethics professionals offer a link to the regulatory world that can allow government regulations to work.

Unlike other types of careers, the field of ethics and compliance is relatively new. It has only recently reached the stage where its practitioners need to define it in ways that can be drawn upon and adhered to. Such consolidation will further aid in attracting new professionals to the occupation. We hope with this book to introduce this new line of work to people who may become the very ones that can help our field grow and succeed.

The field desperately needs strengthening. Certainly, there is strength in numbers, but also, there is strength in community. When practitioners in this field join together and recognize all we have in common, our voices will be louder and our presence unmistakable. In a field so dependent on assertiveness and one's ability to take a stand to defend the ethical choice, be it profitable or not, coming together is not just a one-time goal, but rather an ongoing and never-ending process.

There are people in the business world who simply have jobs—they go to work and get paid. They need that solid job, but perhaps there has always been a desire within them to be something more, to be someone whose concerns and influence go beyond number crunching and profit increases. There are college students who still believe in right and wrong, who have that idealism and optimism. Along the way, however, they feel the tug of the dollar, and wonder if they must sell out to get a good job. There are those in government who would like to move into the business world, but are not sure if their skills apply, or in some cases, if a regulator would be welcomed in among his/her former charges (or victims, depending on the perspective). There are still other people who do not even know this field exists, what it does or how it could fulfill their dreams. Some who know of it underestimate its breadth and potential opportunities, such as those in-house who may not even recognize it is a field and growing profession.

In defining this field, we must pay tribute to the early trailblazers, including leaders such as John Braithwaite of Australian National University—an original and incisive thinker—his protégé Christine Parker, Bill Dee and the late Brian Sharpe, who helped bring the field to Australia. Leaders with whom Joe Murphy, one of the authors, has worked also belong on the list of trailblazers: Jay Sigler, Doug McCollum, Jeff Kaplan, Win Swenson, Kirk Jordan and other professionals who championed and developed this field in its early stages. Also on the list is a cadre of preventive law experts, led by Louis Brown.

We owe special thanks to the pioneers in-house—those doing compliance and ethics work in businesses before anyone even attempted to define the field. We can only guess how many of these worked to keep their companies on the straight and narrow. In Joe Murphy's past, the first actual on-the-job compliance champions he met at Bell were George Glass ("Mr. Clean"), Dan Franceski (the "general trade" guy), and Ed Lowry (the Bell Point of Contact, or "BPOC"). To Joe, a then-young lawyer, seeing such dedication and singular devotion to doing the right thing—even if it alienated superiors or seemed to aid those who competed with the company—opened the door to a whole new way of conducting business.

Such people who worked quietly within large organizations doing difficult (some might even call it heroic) work—they deserve to be recognized, and should find a place in popular culture. We have already witnessed the rise of whistleblowers and crusaders like Erin Brockovich lionized by the media. But it's time for more everyday heroes, the ones who do this job so that the world does not have to depend on frightened whistleblowers and outraged prosecutors. Compliance and ethics professionals do their jobs for the betterment of their companies and their communities, whether or not anybody notices.

We in this field see to it that a working mom comes home from the plant instead of being severely injured by unguarded machinery. We see to it that a long-term, faithful employee nearing retirement is not left without a job and paycheck with his savings wiped out because of some shady corporate accounting scheme. We stop the marketing executive who thinks a little dishonesty will boost the sales results. And though it may lead to fines or bad PR for our employers, we are the ones who insist that an environmental accident be reported to authorities so that damage to the natural environment can be contained and remedied.

We are people who believe an important—even indispensable—part of the answer is strengthened internal systems that use the organization, its people, and its resources to prevent and interdict misconduct. A very tall order, perhaps, and we are not near to this goal yet. Too much wrongdoing still occurs. This field is not yet strong enough to turn the tide, but it can and must be.

This book is an abridged version of a book we wrote offering guidance and examples to those interested in building or enhancing a career in the compliance and ethics field. The full version of the book is entitled *Working for Integrity: Finding the Perfect Job in the Rapidly Growing Compliance and Ethics Field*. You will find more information on that longer text in Appendix F at the end of this book.

It is our hope that these books will help draw the best, brightest, and bravest to this calling. It is also our hope that these books will contribute to the growth of this field, and that they will help lead to more recognition for this profession and those dedicated to its mission.

1   What Is This Field?

What is the field of compliance and ethics?

This book is about exciting employment opportunities in a field that guides and controls organizations to prevent them from doing wrong. This field helps companies and other large institutions to obey the law, act ethically, and avoid harming others. (In this book we sometimes refer to "company" or "companies," but this field applies to *all* organizations, including nonprofits.)

When we speak of ethics and compliance, we are not talking about the course in philosophy that you may have taken in college. In the business world, these topics refer to how people act in large organizations, and how to keep those organizations out of trouble. At the root, we must recognize that organizations act in ways different from individuals, and that individuals in organizations do things that they would not do if acting alone. Those of us working in the field of ethics and compliance seek to prevent organizational misconduct and to protect those who can be harmed by what companies do.

It should be clear that ethics and compliance work is not the practice of law. Of course, major companies have lawyers who advise them on what the law requires. Giving legal advice is part of the traditional role of lawyers. But compliance and ethics work is different. The compliance field deals with how organizations make sure that legal advice is followed. It includes management steps to assure that employees know the rules and do what is right. It also helps bring to the surface legal issues so that managers do, in fact, seek legal advice before they act. The role of lawyers is important in the compliance and ethics field, but this field is much more about how an organization is managed, and not about how laws should be interpreted.

Where did this area come from?

The compliance and ethics field evolved out of the modern corporation. In the twentieth century, the role of large companies became more pronounced and more important in the economy. At the same time, corporations' potential for causing harm also increased. Because of this risk, the government turned to penalties as a way to control wrongdoing in companies and other organizations. Initially, fines and other charges imposed on companies were relatively modest. But in recent years, penalties —including criminal fines, punitive damages and other assessments—have reached into the *billion*-dollar range. In addition, individual company employees and officers also face fines as well as imprisonment for participating in business crimes.

As the attention paid to company misconduct has increased, companies have worked to develop ways to prevent violations from occurring. Initially, specific legal areas were targeted. For example, the 1950s saw the first serious criminal antitrust case against major U.S. companies; thereafter, companies began paying attention to antitrust compliance. Subsequent decades have seen similar reactions to new laws and enforcement efforts in such areas as the environment, employment discrimination, insider trading, overseas payoffs, defense contracting fraud, and recently, accounting fraud.

Because the government directed its enforcement efforts toward specific areas of the law, corporate compliance was viewed in a "stove-pipe" way. A manager responsible for environmental compliance might not realize that similar compliance efforts were happening in other areas such as antitrust or discrimination. Each risk area was dealt with separately. Only gradually did these professionals realize that compliance itself might be a separate subject worth considering on its own.

The real breakthrough in development came in 1991, when the United States Sentencing Commission adopted a set of standards that applies to federal judges sentencing companies and other organizations for federal crimes. (As defined in these standards, an "organization" is any form of group or company imaginable; only individuals are excluded, because there are separate guidelines for them.) To prevent companies from "judge shopping"—finding a judge who would give easy treatment—these standards forced federal judges to be consistent and tough in imposing sentences. These standards, known as the *Federal Sentencing Guidelines*, along with other congressional initiatives, greatly increased penalties for business crimes.

But these new sentencing standards also mandated that judges give a break to companies and other organizations that had in place "effective" compliance programs. The *Federal Sentencing Guidelines* included a set of compliance program standards for judges to apply.[1] The guidelines view compliance as one subject, without regard to any specific area of the law. From 1991 onward this approach took root, and the idea of compliance as a separate field started coming into its own.

What the guidelines set in motion other government agencies and the courts took further. Companies were offered a number of important benefits for implementing effective programs, and for responding the right way whenever they discovered violations. For example, federal prosecutors have stated that they will consider a company's compliance program in deciding whether to criminally prosecute a company, or to give more lenient treatment.

As time has passed since the guidelines took effect in 1991, the standards for compliance programs have evolved. Today compliance practitioners need to know the standards in the *Federal Sentencing Guidelines* (revised in 2004), but they also need to be aware of additional standards that may also apply. While compliance is now accepted as a generic field, there are still differences in emphasis and approach depending on the risk area.[2] For example, environmental compliance may place more emphasis on audits, while compliance regarding sexual and other harassment incidents emphasizes having effective systems for reporting violations and responding effectively.

Compliance standards are also evolving internationally. Some countries, most prominently Australia, have developed standards that apply for all compliance programs. In other areas of the world, such as the European Union, the push has been for compliance programs addressing specific risk areas, such as privacy. The trend is unmistakable, however—compliance programs are a key part of the modern world, and compliance professionals have a future of increasing opportunity in front of them.

If governments resort to increased fines and prison terms for white-collar crime, why is more needed to prevent business misconduct? One reason is that society is not prepared to carry the expense of a government large enough to police all business conduct. The size, number and scope of businesses and other organizations make it unrealistic to rely on outside policing to assure compliance. Even if such a massive governmental effort could work, free societies would not accept the threat posed by such an authoritarian environment.

But there is another, more fundamental reason that after-the-fact enforcement is not sufficient. The legal system, by its very nature, is reactive. Enforcement can only occur after the harm has been done. This may have been an acceptable arrangement when the damage that a company could cause was limited to one small community. But companies today can cause massive harm and disruption. It is unacceptable to wait for such harm to occur before developing preventive steps. Thus, the only realistic alternative is to have internal controls that either prevent compliance disasters, or detect problems early enough to interrupt wrongdoing before it causes great harm. The future of the compliance and ethics field is assured, not just because it is a good idea, but because no other rational alternative exists.

Why do companies and other organizations have compliance programs?

Companies institute compliance programs first and foremost to prevent harm and misconduct from happening. Any rational company will want to prevent the Enron/Andersen-type of meltdowns which can destroy a company. But a whole range of other conduct exists that may not be fatal, but can cause harm to those dealing with the company. These compliance areas include things like ensuring worker safety, avoiding consumer fraud, and protecting the environment.

An effective compliance program can also help protect the company from becoming a victim of someone else's misconduct. For example, a helpline system and a credible investigation system can enable employees to report instances of theft or fraud by other employees or suppliers. Smart compliance audits can detect not only company misconduct, but also such individual crimes as embezzlement.

Preventive programs can also help limit damage to a company's reputation caused by a compliance or ethics scandal. Even if a company has not technically violated the law, a tarnished public image from questionable conduct can cost a company enormous losses in customer, employee and investor loyalty.

Compliance programs also lend credibility to a company if something does go wrong. If a violation of law is unearthed, or company officials are caught in fraudulent conduct, company officials will need to prove to skeptical outsiders that the company was committed to doing the right thing. Increasingly, companies are expected to be good corporate citizens and to join the corporate crime prevention fight. This means having a diligent compliance program and cooperating with government investigators when trouble emerges. In exchange for such responsible corporate actions, companies can receive more lenient treatment from the government and in the courts.

The *Federal Sentencing Guidelines* have provided this incentive for companies to have good compliance programs. Under the guidelines, a company that meets the compliance program standards is entitled to a deep discount in its penalties. In practice, this has happened very infrequently. But the reason for this absence of cases is actually a very positive one. If a company has a good program but nevertheless gets into trouble, the place where the program counts is in negotiating with the government before any trial starts. The U.S. federal government has, for the most part, said that in deciding whether to prosecute it will consider a company's good faith. Whether a company voluntarily comes clean and reports its own violations, or can show the government that it had in place a diligent system to prevent wrongdoing, such positive behavior can have an enormous impact on how it will be treated by regulators and prosecutors.

Why has corporate compliance become so important now? As we stated earlier, big companies can cause massive harm; the larger the company the more damage that can be caused. With such increased risks has arisen an increase in legal regulation, reflecting society's expectations of large organizations. Back when much was done by small, community-based businesses, local communities and peer pressure acted as more of a check on business conduct. But with national and global companies, neighbors are no longer a check on business conduct. Thus it falls to government and the legal system to exert controls.

Concurrently, the standards of acceptable conduct have changed over time. Conduct that was widespread in the past—pollution, employment discrimination, use of customers' private information—has now become unacceptable. Compliance and ethics programs have helped companies adjust to such changing standards of conduct to avoid legal consequences.

Who uses compliance programs?

When we talk about the need for compliance programs, we are not limiting this to specific types or sizes of organizations that require such a program. The *Federal Sentencing Guidelines*, which set the standard for compliance programs, apply to each and every type of organization.

But which organizations have enough legal and ethical risks that they need compliance programs? The answer is exactly the same: It is each and every organization. As long as an organization is made up of human beings there is a risk of bad things happening. The problems may occur from ignorance of the rules, carelessness about what the law requires, or deliberate violations. Wherever there are people there will be risks. Wherever there are risks, organizations need systems and compliance people to control those risks.

Compliance programs are needed in businesses of all kinds, in all industries. The list of industries with compliance scandals seems endless—defense, healthcare, securities, banking, energy, accounting, mutual funds, etc. But compliance programs are also needed in organizational structures beyond the traditional corporation. One need only think of some examples in recent memory. Arthur Andersen, the accounting partnership, was brought down by its involvement in the Enron scandal. The sexual abuse scandals in the Catholic Church were enabled by organizational flaws that could have been remedied with an effective compliance effort. United Way made headlines a few years back because of alleged abuses by its chief officer. The International Olympic Committee made headlines with its ethical failures. Even governments have joined this rogues' list, as shown by scandals in the European Union's own central organization's ranks.

Recent high-profile corporate fraud cases such as Enron and WorldCom have brought attention to the current status of compliance programs in the United States. But the need for compliance efforts clearly crosses all international boundaries. An equally high-profile accounting fraud case involving Italian dairy products giant Parmalat—known as "Europe's Enron"—demonstrates this point. Compliance and ethics programs are needed all around the world, to address all the many areas of legal, ethical, and reputational risk.

What types of risks do compliance programs address?

Risks that need to be addressed by compliance programs fall into three general areas: legal, ethical and reputational risks. The legal category includes criminal areas such as bribery and price fixing, as well as a broad array of non-criminal violations such as employment discrimination and harassment. Ethical concerns and reputational harms are perhaps more difficult to define in a distinct list, but they can be tremendously harmful—both to the organization engaged in misconduct, and to those who may be victims of misconduct.

The line between what is unethical and what is illegal is sometimes blurry and unpredictable. If a company seeks to scrape by doing the minimum the law requires, the odds are fairly high that it will fail in this goal. Those who aim for the bottom tend to miss their low target and eventually break the law. Moreover, law is a flexible concept, and at least in the United States, judges can be quite clever in extending the law to reach sharp practices.

Furthermore, it has been shown employees are more responsive to compliance training that emphasizes "doing the right thing" than to training that explains legal lines. "Doing the right thing" is a much more powerful message than "don't break the law."

There are many types of risks, some dependent on a company's line of business, and some that apply to every organization. Following is one general list, offered just as a guide for understanding the scope of compliance work:

Potential compliance risk areas

- Accounting fraud/earnings management
- Antitrust/competition law
- Federal and state laws requiring compliance programs, e.g., California for pharmaceutical companies
- Confidential information
- Conflicts of interest
- Consent decrees
- Consumer protection/advertising
- Document management/retention
- Employment discrimination/labor law
- Environmental
- Government contracting
- Government investigations/dealings
- Harassment
- Industry-specific (e.g., FCC, FDA)
- Intellectual property
- International (e.g., export, overseas bribery)
- Money laundering
- Political contributions/bribery/lobbying
- Privacy
- Product/service safety
- Purchasing
- Securities law
- Taxes
- Transportation
- Wages and hours/ Fair Labor Standards Act
- Workplace safety and health
- Workplace violence and security

One additional point needs to be noted, before we scare people away from this field. A compliance person would not be expected to know or understand all of these areas. Such breadth of knowledge is up to the lawyers and other subject matter experts. The compliance program does require, however, that the company assess what its risks are and determine how best to prioritize and address them. This is a job for a number of people with the necessary expertise. It is unlikely that any one lawyer, let alone a non-lawyer, could effectively deal with all of these areas without assistance from others.

What is in a compliance program?

All compliance programs must begin with a management commitment to do the right thing. To be more than "just talk," a program must include management steps to make that commitment happen.

What are those management steps? The first point of reference is the standards spelled out in the *Federal Sentencing Guidelines*. These guidelines provide, in a seven-step approach, the touchstone for an effective compliance program.[3]

Although this approach is found in a legal document, it is not legalese. It represents a standard for managing an organization's conduct. It lays out the management steps necessary to prevent and detect as early as possible illegal and unethical conduct. These steps include such things as training, auditing, disciplining people for violations, and—most important for those of us in the compliance and ethics profession—having senior people in charge of the compliance effort to make sure it actually happens.

Note that compliance and ethics programs do not simply rely on good faith. Compliance programs call for the use of strong management techniques plus an element of transparency. For companies to get credit for their programs from the government, for example, they must have diligent programs, and they must be prepared to disclose what they have done. There is no "trust" involved in this process. Moreover, the burden falls fully on the company to *prove* that it has acted in good faith and that its program is genuine.[4]

Throughout the evolution of the compliance and ethics field, a debate continues about whether programs should focus on values and ethics or on law and legal compliance. This controversy has been something of a sideshow, a bit of a tempest in a teapot. As the field has developed, there has been a growing consensus that these two seemingly different approaches really belong together in one subject. Whether called ethics or compliance programs, the programs' purpose and effects are fundamentally the same. Ethics and compliance both require the same careful and diligent management steps in organizations.

Where are the jobs in this field?

Many of the compliance and ethics employment opportunities are found within companies and organizations establishing or operating their own compliance programs. While many if not most of the major, Blue Chip companies have had compliance programs in place for some time, there likely remain many companies that either have not begun programs, or have much more to do in building a creditworthy program.

There are also entire categories of organizations that either have not started the process, or are just getting off the ground. For example, universities (other than university hospitals) have been very late in awakening to the need for compliance programs that cover their operations. Law firms, despite the fact that they advise companies on compliance programs, often have nothing resembling what they tell their own clients to do. Nonprofits, unions and government agencies are all areas of potential future growth for in-house compliance positions. As has been true for other businesses, however, it will likely take compliance disasters that affect them directly before each new category of organization will join this compliance effort. But unless human nature suddenly changes dramatically, it is only a matter of time before these other organizations get burned and decide they, too, need to be serious about compliance and preventive measures.

We cover the available range of positions in later chapters of this book. They include the top compliance position—the chief compliance or ethics officer in the company—down to the compliance support staff. Many of these people only work on compliance part time, but there are a variety of positions where the predominant, and sometimes exclusive, role is compliance. We also cover all the work that is done to ensure compliance in each of the risk areas such as antitrust, discrimination, environmental protection, and privacy.

While most compliance positions are in-house, a growing market of service providers has developed to help companies meet their compliance objectives. These jobs are also covered in detail in later chapters. Among the service providers are ethics and compliance consultants, lawyers, accountants and investigators. There are also companies that provide online training, and companies that provide services such as helpline and hotline offerings. In these companies the positions may range from administrative and management jobs found in any company, to specialized positions calling for substantive compliance expertise.

Will compliance and ethics programs prevent corporate crime?

The rapid development of this field and its potential to prevent great harm are exciting. But there must always be an element of realism in approaching the challenges of company crime and misconduct. A strong compliance program can prevent and detect much wrongdoing. However, it must be remembered that large, multinational companies are organizations with employee numbers that rival the populations of cities. Just as no city would expect to prevent or even solve all crimes, it is naive to think that even the best compliance program will prevent all problems. There can never be a complete guarantee of success.

But with that caveat, there is cause for hope in this field. A good, empowered program can help set the culture in a company or other organization to resist the types of schemes that characterized business crime in the Enron Era. A strong, well-designed program that has the support of an informed and independent board of directors can stand in the way of even determined and powerful corporate criminals. In those tests of strength when a forceful top executive pushes to have things done his or her way without the interference of others, protecting the company and the public will ultimately rely on the character and persistence of the compliance person. The most exciting message of this book is that you could be that person who makes a difference.

Endnotes

1. See Appendix B: "Sentencing Guidelines Definition," for a discussion of this topic. The Guidelines are no longer mandatory for federal judges, but remain as a key factor in sentencing.
2. For more information about effective compliance and ethics programs, read Joseph E. Murphy, *Compliance Primer: A Guide to the World of Compliance and Ethics Programs* (Waltham, Mass.: Integrity Interactive), and refer to Appendix C in this book, entitled: "Where Can I Get More Information and Advice?"
3. See Appendix B: "Sentencing Guidelines Definition," for the specific steps.
4. For the very serious reader, we recommend Jeffrey M. Kaplan, Joseph E. Murphy and Winthrop M. Swenson, editors, *Compliance Programs and the Corporate Sentencing Guidelines: Preventing Criminal and Civil Liability* (Eagan, Minn.: Thomson/West, 1993).

2

Why Should I Go Into This Field?

Is compliance and ethics a field you should consider for your career? What is it about this subject that draws people to it? Does it make sense from a practical perspective? Is it financially rewarding? Will it be a personal match for your talents and disposition? We address here some of the answers to these questions. We start with the practical and financial reasons, and then move to the intangibles that so many in this field find appealing.[1]

Practical reasons

A growing field

One of the most important practical questions about any career choice is whether the field is dynamic or static. Is this a dead-end line of pursuit, or is there room to grow and prosper into the future?

It is probably obvious to all who follow the news that business misconduct has attracted considerable attention in the past few years. But is the public's focus on business misconduct a short-term phenomenon? Beyond the media attention for major criminal fraud cases like Enron and Parmalat, there lies a longer-term and unmistakable trend: a push to create more reform and controls, and a greater push to have organizations take steps to respond.

Well before Enron became a synonym for business misconduct, waves of scandal in different compliance areas happened. Just a few examples make the point: the defense industry scandals of the 80s, healthcare fraud cases in the 90s, insider trading scandals, options backdating—the list has no end. While it is likely that no one can, with certainty, predict where the next major scandal will occur, we can all safely predict that there will be another one, and more after that. These scandals will bring more calls for compliance and ethics professionals who can help companies develop the tools they need to clean up the mess and restore trust. The specific areas of focus may vary based on the types of violations at issue—e.g., privacy, product safety, environmental safety, etc.,—but the overall pattern is consistent.

This field is not only expanding (in terms of demand) in specific risk areas, it is also expanding on a global basis. Whether it is required privacy officers in Germany, or codes of conduct mandated for listed companies by the Securities and Exchange Board of India (SEBI), this trend has taken root in the business environment around the world. Increasingly, compliance and ethics professionals in one country can find their counterparts to network with in other countries, from Australia to France, and from India to South Africa.

Compliance jobs are now beginning to receive media attention. In fact, the role of compliance officer has actually made it into some lists of "hottest jobs." Thus far, the authors have seen no reliable assessments of the size of the market, although we have developed an estimate of 150,000–250,000 full and part-time compliance and ethics positions, and growing.

Every now and then, a speaker in the compliance and ethics field will opine that the job of the compliance person is to "work yourself out of a job." This statement is usually meant in a very theoretical way: that our job is to establish such an effective system that compliance people will no longer be needed. A few, however, may actually believe that compliance as a function will ultimately be taken over completely by other business managers, and there will be no need for compliance professionals. This view is reminiscent of Karl Marx's ill-conceived notion that the state would just "wither away" once his vision of a collectivist utopia was achieved. Neither event will happen, at least not in the lifetimes of anyone who is reading this book.

What is particularly odd about this "work yourself out of a job" notion is that it doesn't extend to the profession established to deal most frequently with conflict—the legal profession *never* makes this type of assertion. No one realistically thinks that we will find methods for resolving all forms of conflict between humans, so we know we will continue to need the legal system to address and resolve these disputes. And just as the legal system will require legal professionals to operate, so too, compliance and ethics programs will require trained professionals who know how to energize and guide them.

There will always be conflicts when the relative single-mindedness of organizations' goals conflict with the differing agendas of society. Compliance and ethics people are needed to assure there are processes in organizations to navigate these areas of conflict, and, in a very real sense, represent society's larger values within the particular organization. In addition, compliance and ethics professionals will always be needed to deal with the vagaries of human nature—

people's weaknesses and misconduct. Just as lawyers know these forces are not going to fade away, so compliance and ethics people recognize that their jobs are a necessary part of the landscape.

Furthermore, the field of compliance and ethics is not cyclical. It is not tied to economic cycles like other businesses. In good times and bad, human misconduct exists. In good times people get greedy. In bad times they get desperate. In truth, it is best not to spend a great deal of energy trying to predict when misconduct will occur. Just know that the need for compliance and ethics programs is not driven by the usual business cycles.

There are, however, important drivers in this field. They are the government agencies and enforcement officials, activist non-governmental organizations, and plaintiffs' lawyers. They are also the reporters and journalists who look for the next business headline. The people who move the compliance market are constantly watching and taking action to address perceived missteps. Each time a new scandal breaks they are there to push the bar higher for organizations, with the full backing of the increasingly attentive public.

An important point for those in the field of compliance and ethics, however, stems from the public's tendency to focus on specific areas of compliance. One needs to exercise care in selecting a compliance and ethics specialty, and to not limit one's scope too narrowly. There is certainly benefit in mastering a specialty area, but care should be taken. By choosing a narrow specialty in compliance and ethics, one risks becoming outdated by shifts in the field and the perceived needs for particular specialties.

A good job

Compliance, then, is a field with good prospects for the future. It is also an area that offers good jobs in Blue Chip companies. Consider the names of companies on the membership lists of organizations like the Ethics and Compliance Officers' Association (ECOA, formerly EOA) and Society of Corporate Compliance and Ethics (SCCE), or on the customer lists of the online compliance training providers: IBM, Coca-Cola, Alcoa, UTC, Microsoft, DuPont. Large, established companies, dynamic growing market leaders, companies that are rated the best employers—all need compliance and ethics people. With companies of this caliber come the types of pay and benefits that are identified with leading businesses. The companies with the strongest commitments to ethical business are also the ones most respected in their communities.

Among the potential benefits of working in this field, compliance is also a line of pursuit that offers the opportunity to travel. Wherever the company does business it needs to be concerned with compliance issues. Some of the most crucial compliance functions—training, conducting reviews, interviewing witnesses in investigations—typically require travel to the business' locations. As a compliance lawyer in one company, for example, Joe Murphy spent time in such diverse locations as New Zealand, the Czech Republic, Paris, Mexico City, and Minot, North Dakota. The impetus for establishing diligent compliance programs is spreading around the world, so travel will likely continue to be an option for compliance and ethics practitioners. Furthermore, the global environment also presents the opportunity for job assignments in foreign locales, especially since many large corporations like to circulate their managers and officers (including those working in compliance) to their foreign offices.

Personal development opportunities

Compliance and ethics is an exceedingly broad field, calling for a wide variety of skills. Compliance and ethics people teach, manage, investigate, advocate, motivate, write, communicate, analyze and apply many other skills in achieving their objectives. This is a field in which you can develop skills that would serve you well in a full range of activities in a company.

Being in compliance and ethics also means that you get to see and experience many parts of a business. For example, in order to be an effective trainer it is important to know your audience and what they do in their jobs. So, just conducting a training course for sales people means you have the opportunity to learn what the sales team must know, and experience what they experience. Each group you train brings a chance to learn more about the business. As any experienced trainer can tell you, one key to effective training is the willingness to remain open to learning. As a compliance trainer, you will be constantly learning about those you train.

Compliance and ethics work also involves auditing and investigating operations in the business. These processes immerse you in intensive learning experiences. For example, if you are called upon to audit the purchasing operation in the UK, you will need to know how that unit operates, what is considered normal practice, and what would be acceptable. You need to know who is who, and what the expected practices are in purchasing. This provides a highly valuable window for seeing how various parts of the business operate. Thus, even if your ultimate career goals are outside of compliance, time in this field allows you to shop around the business to see what really interests you. If your goal is to advance in compliance, you will still find it invigorating to learn about all the challenges that occur in other parts of the business. Either way, you will make many contacts and gain much knowledge through your networking efforts.

Compliance and ethics work not only gives you the opportunity to see many parts of your own company's operations, it also allows you to examine the many subject areas that are part of compliance. Consider the list of risks faced by the typical business or other organization: environmental protection, workplace safety, overseas bribery, antitrust, privacy, employment discrimination, consumer protection—the list is practically endless. Each of these risk areas has its own base of knowledge that a practitioner must master. Being in compliance gives you a window into these different areas. You can dip into the fast-developing area of privacy, or learn about the science involved in environmental protection. You can examine the economics behind antitrust standards, or study the cultural elements behind overseas bribery. There is no need to stand still in this field—every day brings new occasions to learn a new area, or observe new developments in any of these subject areas.

Even though compliance and ethics can involve some of the most challenging subject areas, this is one field where an advanced degree or state licensure is simply not required. It is true that only a lawyer can practice law and give legal advice in the legal areas; it is also true that different compliance areas may have special requirements for practice in those fields. And there is certainly an advantage to being a lawyer or having relevant areas of expertise and professional status. But pursuing a career in compliance and ethics simply requires skills a good manager should have—motivational, communication, project management, etc.—this is a field that is wide open to those with the right level of commitment.

For those considering their career options, the good news about the compliance and ethics field is that it is open to newcomers. You can learn this field on the job. Being a good compliance manager certainly takes work. But you can enter this field without a professional degree. You can learn from reading the materials published by practitioners. You can learn from networking with those working in this field. Rather than full degree programs, you can take short external courses and seminars that cover the basics. If you can get an advanced degree such as a law degree there is no question that this helps, but it is not essential. You can be a star in a company's compliance and ethics program with a four-year college degree and well-developed corporate street smarts.

The opportunities are also not limited to in-house positions. You can do consulting on compliance and ethics programs without a law degree and without being a CPA. Because the focus is business management, management experience, skills and techniques are essential ingredients. If you can apply good management practices in the compliance and ethics context, and if you are a creative problem solver, then you can help companies and build a viable business.

For those who have started their careers in the enforcement/regulatory world, note that an enforcement background is very useful for entering compliance and ethics. One reason companies establish a compliance and ethics program is to demonstrate to the government that the organization is committed to doing the right thing. If a company has a former enforcement person on its compliance team, this can reinforce the message that the company is serious about its commitment to compliance. The former enforcement person also has an enormous advantage in having the ability to see things from the government's perspective. Who better to convince managers of the government's expectations regarding compliance programs than someone who has sat on the other side of the table? For a company trying to ensure that it has a credible program, having an internal devil's advocate is highly valuable.

For the government person entering the business world, compliance work offers a smooth transition. You can still be devoted to ensuring that people do the right thing, but at the same time you can learn about the business world from inside. You can apply skills you have spent years developing in the government, but also learn about this new world of business. Instead of beating companies on the head from the outside, you can work from the inside on practical ways to make things better.

One other practical advantage that comes to all who enter the compliance and ethics area: it is a field that's still maturing, and you can grow with it. While this field is no longer in its infancy, it is still young and developing. Even someone new to the field can take on projects and analyses that others have not done. If you bring a special perspective or area of expertise, you may be the one who sees things that others have overlooked. It is still early enough to influence the development of techniques and approaches to compliance, and to grow with this field as it expands.

Advancement and mobility

For those who are looking for personal development, or a field where they are doing the right thing, the advantages of compliance and ethics are obvious. But if your objective is rapid advancement and mobility—the ability to climb to the top of the economic ladder rapidly—then you may want to apply a more careful review.

The history of the field teaches us that compliance and ethics work does not offer the short route to becoming chairman of the board in large companies.

Will this trend likely change? There is certainly reason to doubt it. The compliance person is typically not a person who has the making of money as his or her first priority. This person does not usually generate the most revenue, nor cut costs most effectively, nor lead an entire business unit. Perhaps this connection could exist some day, but it will not happen anytime soon. Having said this, however, there are, in fact, instances of crossovers, where a business unit head in one company has become the compliance person in another.

Setting aside the hope for a rapid route to the corporate pinnacle—the CEO's position—there is a route in compliance and ethics that can lead to a position as one of the top executives at a company. This route takes one to the chief compliance officer position.[2] The compliance officer in companies that are serious about compliance will be a senior officer in the top echelons. He or she will need to have direct access to the chief executive officer. Whenever a senior level meeting is held the compliance officer should also be there. If the person is truly empowered there will be direct access to the board of directors. As company boards become more concerned about corporate wrongdoing and their own potential liability, they will likely see the need to assure the status of the chief compliance officer. They will insist on having a compliance officer with the clout to prevent misconduct at all levels of the business. In the future, as the field of compliance broadens, the route to the top compliance position may draw increasingly on those who have gathered long-term experience in this field, and are recognized as true compliance professionals.

We can also anticipate that compliance may become one of the steps on the way to other senior management positions. GE has been noted as a company where service in internal audit is used as a stage for advancement—a ticket that needs to be punched. In time, companies that want to be identified as leaders in compliance and ethics may well adopt this same philosophy for compliance functions. They may encourage those on the fast track to executive leadership to take a turn in the compliance and ethics organization. Companies that want to prevent misconduct may see enormous benefit in ensuring that managers pick up the compliance perspective as part of their advancement in the company.

In addition to considering the route to the top of the corporate organization, one should look at beginning and intermediate career prospects in compliance and ethics. In the earliest days of the field, when it appeared that companies with a compliance or ethics officer were far in front of the others, not many prospects existed. Having only one slot in a company with 200,000 employees would not appear to provide very favorable odds. But the field has changed dramatically and moved away from those early roots. Today there are numerous positions that share the compliance and ethics mission in the typical large organization. There may be a compliance central staff, coordinator positions throughout the field organization, compliance auditors in internal audit, investigators in security, subject matter experts in the legal department, EEO experts in human resources, privacy officers—the list goes on and on. A serious potential exists for companies to develop compliance and ethics career tracks. Capable, determined people could be groomed to advance and grow in this part of the business.

In addition, there is still room for an entrepreneurial person to open new markets, and provide new, needed services. The rules and requirements from government keep evolving, and the opportunities for misconduct by employees, suppliers, and others in the corporate world seem to grow continuously. This leaves open the door for clever people to identify new markets and opportunities to provide compliance-related products and services.

One need only look at the new regulations established in the Sarbanes-Oxley Act to see this phenomenon in action. There are now consultants, lawyers, and software experts offering their services to meet this challenge. We can all rest assured that new challenges will come with the next set of corporate corruption headlines. Such unknowns will keep the business world in turmoil and continue to keep the compliance and ethics field a dynamic one.

The pursuit of vigorous compliance work also offers opportunities to get close to other parts of the business. Whether it is field training visits, or compliance audits, or in-depth investigations, interactive compliance work can get one into other parts and functions of the business. This work offers a window to learn about a broad range of activities in the business. Similarly, taking a position as a field compliance officer in one of the company's business units may introduce one to new parts of the company.

Another element of mobility can come from having a compliance background. Companies that have had legal troubles typically crave anything that helps them restore their credibility. A person who has held a compliance and ethics role in another company holds great appeal for a company that is looking to reform itself.

Compliance and ethics, then, may not be the short route to becoming the next Donald Trump. But for an ambitious person who seeks expanding opportunities, it can hold more than enough promise of success.

Personal reasons

While we deliberately chose to focus first on practical reasons to consider the compliance and ethics field, the strongest reasons for pursuing it will probably always be the personal gratification that this field brings to those who believe in it.

Being proud at the end of the day

At the end of a day at work, what does the average person take home besides another day's pay? In the compliance and ethics field, we have the knowledge that we have spent our day trying to do the right thing. We train employees so that they avoid getting into trouble. We help them protect customers who otherwise might be injured by our companies' products. We help them avoid being the target of a government investigation. We help them deal honestly with customers, and deal carefully with the environment.

Doing a compliance job diligently and honestly means never becoming another Willy Loman in *Death of a Salesman*, who spends his mediocre life selling products for an ungrateful employer. While we work to promote the interests of our employers, we also have a duty to act according to a higher standard that considers the interests of the public and the requirements of the law.

Helping protect people

Compliance and ethics people help other people avoid mistakes that can ruin their careers. A great deal of this work is done by providing training and offering examples of others' mistakes to serve as lessons on how to avoid the same pitfalls. When an employee reads a compliance news bulletin about a senior manager "electing to resign" after a conflict of interest investigation, that employee might be inspired to voluntarily disclose and discuss his or her own potential conflict, thus saving an otherwise promising career. When a worker sees a company videotape showing how an accident occurred at an operation just like his or hers, that worker may be motivated to take that one extra step that saves a lifetime of regret.

Those in this profession also help prevent others from being harmed by the company's misconduct. Who could forget the retirees from companies like Enron and WorldCom, wondering how they were going to get by when their life savings had been wiped out by corporate corruption? Compliance people know they do not have to sit idly by being mere witnesses to such harm and personal devastation. Those in this field know that they are there to prevent just this type of disaster from happening.

One example experienced by one of the authors illustrates this point. Author Joe Murphy was the recipient of a call from a scared junior employee who feared his boss was intent on doing something wrong that would also involve him. The caller was too scared at first to reveal his name or any identifying information. This reluctance was understandable—he was one of only three people in his business unit, and the other two were already involved in the suspect activity. By giving this person a bit of comfort and counsel, the author was able to pursue a course that ended well for all. The junior employee checked on a few matters suggested in the call and determined, to his relief, that he had misunderstood some elements involved, and he had nothing to worry about. Even in this case, where no harm had actually been threatened to third parties, it was entirely gratifying to be able to help someone in great stress to reach a resolution. This sense of satisfaction is even greater when the result is to avoid actual harm, or to ferret out wrongdoing at an early stage, before great harm can result.[3]

An interesting and dynamic subject

Not only is this field dynamic in terms of its growth around the world, but the subject itself is an interesting one that keeps changing with the times. New risks will continue to appear on the business horizon. History teaches us that those who are intent on wrongdoing are alarmingly creative. Compliance people are charged with handling such negative creativity—testing systems, tracking the flow of money and other valuable resources in the company, looking for ways that misconduct can occur. Each violation uncovered may reveal weaknesses in existing systems while reminding the compliance person of the need for constant vigilance.

A dedicated compliance person will have little opportunity for moments of self-satisfaction; he or she will be busy attending programs on new developments, and networking with peers in other companies who are developing yet new approaches to training, auditing, providing incentives, or one of the myriad other elements of a compliance and ethics effort.

Compliance and ethics involves dealing with real people with real, and sometimes daunting, concerns. On this level particularly, work in this field can be quite exciting and challenging. The next phone call or email could change everything you were doing at that time. You could be off on a jet to India, or heading up an investigation team to meet with a senior vice president. Your work might take you to a remote manufacturing facility or into a meeting with the top sales executives.

Working in this field gives you a fascinating study of human nature. On a day-to-day basis, you see people at their best and their worst. You will try to figure out why an executive being paid millions of dollars a year, and widely respected by thousands of employees, would foolishly try to cheat the company out of a few expense dollars. You will face an honored member of the community who tries to coerce a young, vulnerable employee into unwanted sexual contact. You will delve into why a small foreign unit would risk everything by paying bribes to buy off a tax collector. You will find yourself wondering what makes people in groups do things that none of them individually would do.

Yet at the same time you will see everyday heroes. You will meet the plant employee who insists on reporting a hazardous work condition to protect his or her follow workers. You will come into contact with the sales manager who passes up a chance to gain a marketing advantage and instead calls the legal department after receiving a competitor's secret business plans from some anonymous source. You will hear from people who know it is risky in any organization to blow the whistle, but are genuinely angered that someone in their company is cheating customers and endangering the company's good name.

Like so much of the business world today, this line of business is also heavily affected by technology. Years ago, for example, training involved the use of a VCR and an overhead projector. Now training involves advanced software systems, in-house webinars, and the widespread reach of online training tools. In the past, keeping track of calls to the helpline might have been the job of an administrative assistant checking in by phone with the field investigators. Today there are sophisticated tracking systems that pull together all pending matters and even remind participants when appropriate actions need to be taken. Tomorrow we can expect still more systematic approaches to solving compliance challenges.

Having said these positive things about this type of work, we should remind readers that the work is quite difficult and challenging. While it does not carry the dangers involved in police work (odds are you will not be shot in the back in a dark alley), it does have all the dangers inherent in the business world (a compliance person caught off guard may well be "stabbed in the back" in the office corridors). Expect that there will be pressure to perform, and confrontations with others in the organization. Politics is an essential part of compliance work—the ability to get others to conform to your agenda is a necessity in compliance. Crises can emerge that will test your ability to make difficult decisions with little time for reflection. You will not have many relaxing hours on this job, but for those cut out for the field, the positives outweigh those challenges.

Why not become a prosecutor or trial lawyer?

If you are inclined to champion law and order and to fight against wrongdoing, then you might reasonably ask, why not just become a prosecutor or regulatory trial lawyer? Why not spend your time in court getting juries to convict the bad actors—won't that teach them all a lesson and stop corporate crime in its tracks?

Without question, government enforcement efforts will continue to be needed no matter how much attention companies pay to compliance. Even the best compliance program cannot claim it will always prevent wrongdoing. But one must consider the major differences between the work of a prosecutor and the work of the compliance person, and then an informed choice can be made.

First and most fundamental, compliance and ethics people help *prevent* misconduct. Law enforcement is only called in after the violation occurs and the harm has been done. Compliance and ethics, on the other hand, exists for the very purpose of anticipating what may go wrong and preventing it from happening at all. We do not wait for failure before we institute corrective measures. We test for weaknesses, look for minor violations that could ripen into disasters, and strive every day to keep things working right. And when things do go wrong, it is the compliance practitioner's job to discover the flawed policies and practices that allowed or facilitated the wrongdoing, and to work to prevent such misconduct from occurring again.

In addition to the essentially reactive nature of the legal system, a prosecutor's work is centered on the idea of controlled conflict. The ideal of the trial is that two competing forces clash, and truth is discovered in that conflict. But whether truth emerges, or the parties merely settle on the best terms they can get, it is intended as a win-lose system. When someone wins, someone else loses. Lawyers are ethically charged to pursue their clients' interests with "zeal." In effect, it is a system designed to replace actual physical violence with a substitute form of verbal conflict as a means for resolving disputes. Compliance and ethics, on the other hand, is not a child of conflict. Rather, it is a civilized society's means to prevent harm being caused by organizations. It does not succeed by pitting combatants against each other, but rather by encouraging the best possible conduct by those in business.

In considering a legal career it is also important to distinguish between Hollywood and the real world. The legal system is fraught with ambiguity, delay and pressure. In fact, many would say that delay is a core tactic of the legal system. If wearing down an opponent through delay is likely to improve one's negotiating position, then the system seems to lend itself to that use. Ask any lawyer, and you'll hear about the years of discovery and motion practice in litigation, about the lengthy, painstaking detail involved in the litigation process. All of these litigation scars are part of what compliance people work to avoid. When we can keep good people out of litigation, we count that a major success.

For those who see a career in law as an opportunity to be a knight riding to the rescue of the downtrodden, the legal system can be a sharp disappointment. Those who have experienced the process may bemoan a system that can be counterproductive, exploiting good compliance efforts for the sake of litigation strategy. A company's own internal investigations, its code of conduct, its compliance training materials—all are treated as mere tools for use by adversaries in the game of litigation.

In contrast, compliance people work behind the scenes. Compliance and ethics work is usually much less exciting; this is not the place for the person who likes to grandstand. But it is an opportunity to pursue true crime-prevention, even detective work, while still being paid well. Your job is not to give stirring speeches to a jury in order to convict some malefactor. Instead, your job is to prevent the harm in a much more direct way than any legal system could achieve.

The nature of the people in this field

Of the factors that make this line of work so appealing, one of the most important and gratifying to compliance and ethics professionals is the nature of the people in this field. Compliance and ethics is an open field, where the model relies on the sharing of best practices and consulting one another about our experiences. Compliance people freely network with their peers, and seek opportunities to share their experiences and discoveries. Large organizations, such as the Society of Corporate Compliance and Ethics, have formed simply because compliance and ethics practitioners want to have places to share ideas and support each other.

Compliance and ethics people believe in doing the right thing—that is their job. Many of these people consider this career a calling. They believe in what they are doing, even when other managers in their companies challenge whether they are "going overboard." The team orientation within the compliance/ethics community therefore offers a great source of strength and support for those who enter this field.

Appendix 2A

Should I Go into Compliance and Ethics?
Some Questions to Ask Yourself

- Do you want to enter a field that is still growing, where one person can make a difference in the development of the whole field?
- Do you like teaching adults, and explaining difficult rules or concepts to people?
- Are you interested in what makes people in organizations do what they do?
- Do you think it is possible to "do good" and "do well" at the same time, i.e., do things that help others and get compensated well for it?
- Are you willing to stand up for what is right when everyone else wants to just "go along"?
- Do you resist rationalizing doing something wrong just because someone higher up says to do so?
- Do you want a job that allows you to make a difference in the world?
- Do you want a job where people at other companies network to freely share their experiences with you?
- Do you want a job where you can travel?

If you answer "yes," to the above questions, that is a sign that compliance might be right for you. Now try these:

- Do you believe people have to sacrifice their ethics and values to succeed in business?
- Do you believe the only purpose of any business is to make money?
- Do you believe that in business it is ok to bend the rules or dodge the law if necessary to get results?
- Do you assume that people will always do the right thing, left to their own devices?
- Are you looking for a quiet way to make a living while you pursue your hobbies and other interests outside of the workplace?
- Do you need clear, measurable, bottom line results that show you contributed to your employer's quarterly earnings?

If you found yourself saying "yes" to these questions, then compliance would not be a comfortable fit for you.

Compliance people are not cynics, but they also know a bit about human nature. They are also comfortable with some degree of ambiguity about what results they can achieve, but can take great satisfaction in knowing that they may be helping employees and others do the right thing and stay out of trouble.

Endnotes

1. To help you weigh whether or not Compliance and Ethics is a good field for you, see Appendix 2A: "Should I go into Compliance and Ethics? Some Questions to Ask."
2. See Chapter 5: "The Top Job In-House: Compliance Officer."
3. For anyone who might forget the types of terrible disasters that can occur when there is no such corporate sentinel, we recommend reading Russell Mokhiber's *Corporate Crime and Violence: Big Business Power and the Abuse of the Public Trust* (New York: Random House, 1988). While this perspective could be considered anti-corporate, its examples serve as a graphic reminder of why this field and those who practice in it are so important, and why this work gives its adherents a sense of purpose.

3   How Do I Get Into This Field?

You have decided that this might be the field for you. The question then becomes how to make the transition. We will look here primarily at two approaches, one from a position inside a company, and the other from school. We recommend that those still in school also read the discussion on starting from inside a company, since some of these points may prove helpful for the student. (Chapter 6, "Careers in Compliance for Lawyers," covers this transition for those in the legal profession.) For a checklist of steps to enhance your resume, see Appendix 3A: "Resume Builders: Things You Can Do to Advance in the Compliance and Ethics Field."

Starting from inside a company

You have been working in a job that leaves you cold or presents no opportunity for growth. Maybe you are currently in finance, or in sales, or in purchasing; perhaps you are on the professional staff: a company lawyer, accountant or auditor. Whatever your situation, you are at a point where you want to consider making the switch into the field of compliance and ethics.

Your present position should not hinder your considerations; nevertheless, given the nature of the field, it is an easier transition for those with management experience than for those in non-management positions. However, there is no barrier for making the switch if you are persistent and willing to learn a new area.

Networking inside your company

Square one for making the transition is to examine the makeup of your own company's compliance and ethics program. In taking this step, you will learn early on one of the significant characteristics of this field—networking is a core part of compliance and ethics. People in this field appreciate a sympathetic ear, someone who is interested in what compliance folks do and what the field is about. Showing interest can make it easier to chat with compliance and ethics practitioners.

First, you will want to master some of the background. Take the time to learn about your own company's compliance program. To approach this learning, you will need to know some basics about compliance and how compliance programs work. A number of outside sources are available.[1]

But where do you begin with your company's compliance program? The logical starting point is to read and understand your code of conduct. Companies typically treat this element as the foundation of their program, covering the most important risk areas and explaining at least some of their compliance policies. As an employee, you should already have a copy of the code, but be sure you have the most up-to-date version. If you work for a company listed on the New York Stock Exchange, your current code will also be on the company's public Website. Spend some time becoming familiar with the code and you will be more comfortable when you talk with your company's compliance people. If your company posts its code on its Website, you may also find additional information there about the compliance program. Be sure to become familiar with this material, too.

Most companies with compliance programs also have helplines through which employees can ask questions and raise concerns. If you have a question about the code, try out the helpline to see how it works. Be sure it is a serious question—do not ask something trivial just for the experience. Most codes cover a number of difficult issues, and if you test out different scenarios, you should be able to readily come up with questions that could use clarification.

Another basic step is to take advantage of the compliance training your company offers. Contact whoever is responsible for compliance in your business unit and ask about what training is available. While some of it may be specialized, there are always subjects, like those relating to mutual respect and conflicts of interest, that will apply to all employees. Be sure to explore any online library materials associated with the training.

Once you have learned more about the field, you might consider volunteering to help with the compliance effort in your business unit. Depending on the size of your business unit, the compliance functions may well be part time—just additions to someone's existing job. Volunteering to help out can provide you early experience in the compliance area. Such work might include helping to organize training sessions, assuring that compliance materials have been properly distributed, participating in organizing a local compliance committee, or even assisting in the thankless task of managing records retention.

With this preparation, you are now in a good position to network with the people in your company who run the compliance program. Ask to meet with those in the program to learn about what they do and what they are planning for the compliance program. During these discussions it will become clear that you share their interest in the field. Developing these social contacts within the compliance program will help put your name at the top of the list of candidates for compliance work. This is a field where just expressing an interest and knowing something about the field can get you noticed.

You should also look for opportunities to get outside training in this field,[2] develop outside contacts, and network in the compliance and ethics field. These steps and others discussed below will help you advance from the initial steps here.

Networking outside your company

Whether you only want to work in compliance within your current company or at other companies, networking with compliance and ethics people from other companies is an important step. For those interested in considering other companies, networking is a key step for making the move.

How do you begin networking? Accomplishing this goal is easier in compliance than it may be in other fields, because people tend to be fairly open in this field. One reason for this openness can be found in the Sentencing Guidelines.[3] The Guidelines require company programs to be at least as good as "industry practice." In order to have a feel for industry practice, it is necessary to communicate with compliance practitioners at other companies.

Another reason for the prevalence of networking relates to the nature of this subject area. Compliance and ethics work in a company is seen as different from other functions. Because part of the job may have you operating as a kind of traffic cop, you are less likely to be seen as a regular team member. Thus compliance people may feel a bit more disconnected from their fellow workers, or at least have a sense that they are somewhat different. On the other hand, when they network with their counterparts at other companies, they have the sense that they are with kindred spirits. A compliance manager at one company can reassure a counterpart going through a crisis that, in fact, this is a normal event and that the compliance person is right in his or her perspective. Compliance practitioners in different companies tend to look to their counterparts for important validation.

One step toward networking is to subscribe to publications in the compliance and ethics field. When you read a publication like *ethikos,* or *Compliance & Ethics*, note the authors who make points that interest you—then contact the authors with your comments, questions and suggestions. Most writers find that they get very little feedback from their published pieces. To have a reader contact the author and demonstrate that the article was engaging will usually catch the attention of the writer—you may be able to establish an ongoing discourse with him or her. This process can open a door to getting deeper into this field.

Today it is quite common for companies to obtain compliance services from outside vendors. These may be online training providers, helpline operators, software providers, consultants, etc. Find out if your company uses one or more of these vendors and, if so, develop contacts with them. Like company compliance people, they will usually appreciate your interest in this field and may help you in learning more about the industry. They may even have first-hand knowledge of job openings among their client base.

Like other fields, this one has produced various organizations and forums where participants meet and share information and experiences. Some of these organizations handle special areas, while others embody the entire field. In the United States, the Society of Corporate Compliance and Ethics (SCCE) and the Ethics & Compliance Officer Association (ECOA)[4] are the primary organizations for ethics and compliance workers. Appropriately, they hold membership meetings that provide learning opportunities about this field.

If your interests gravitate toward health care, the Health Care Compliance Association (HCCA) is open to anyone who shares the interest in compliance. Like ECOA and SCCE, HCCA holds national conferences and meetings. Additionally, it has regional chapters that provide the opportunity for networking. Even if you are not already involved in compliance, you can join, although you might have to pay for membership yourself if your employer has not yet given you compliance responsibilities.

Other organizations may focus on specific functions or risk areas. For example, the International Association of Privacy Professionals deals with compliance in the privacy sector, and the International Ombuds Association covers only those who function in an ombuds position. Organizations similar to SCCE and ECOA exist around the world, such as the Australasian Compliance Institute in Australia and the Ethics and Compliance and Custodian Organization (ECCO) in South Africa.

Whichever of these organizations you join, plan to use them as much as possible. Attend the meetings and training programs they provide so you can learn more and make new contacts. Get in touch with the organizations themselves to see what services they offer, and mention that you are looking for an opening in this field.

In addition to these general groups, there are also smaller groups, or compliance forums, that are less formal. These are typically either based on a specific industry, or cover one geographic area. For example, there is a compliance forum in the pharmaceutical industry that meets twice a year. There are geographically based groups in such cities as Boston, Atlanta, Houston, San Francisco, and Seattle. While membership in these forums is by company, you might be able to prevail on your company's compliance staff to allow you to attend at least one of the meetings. Such forums can be an excellent source of information about openings in your industry or locale.

Getting into this field from school

Suppose you are a student in a university considering career options, and think compliance and ethics might fit your strengths. What route should you take to reach this objective? It may be useful to take a two-level approach. The first, and most obvious, is as a student considering how best to prepare for a specific job market. But the second is to remember that, like the company employee looking to move into this field, your college or university may well have a compliance program. We will consider that aspect first.

Although compliance efforts have been going on for decades, one of the last frontiers in the United States seems to be academia, or at least the part of academia not associated with health care (teaching hospitals have already been the focus of strong enforcement actions on the Medicare/Medicaid front and will likely already be compliance true believers). Universities are subject to most of the same compliance risks faced by companies, as well as special risks that apply to them.[5] However, until very recently, universities generally did not seem to recognize the need for compliance programs, and were notably absent from the field (except for their faculty advising others how to develop ethics and compliance programs).

A student interested in this field could first inquire of his or her own school to determine what it does in this area. This effort may take some digging, since few may be aware of the university's compliance work. But even universities without a full-scale compliance and ethics program will typically have done work toward environmental compliance, worker safety, and discrimination/harassment prevention. You may have to reach out to the school's auditors, human resources department or facilities administrators to learn anything in this area.

In addition to learning what your university is currently doing, you can obtain firsthand experience by taking on the role of champion of compliance and ethics efforts at your university. This work may put you in an adversarial role with others at the school, but that in itself would present a useful learning experience. Before tackling this objective, you will first want to learn more about the compliance field, as well as what other universities are doing. But with that background, you may find opportunities to take initiative that you might not find in the business world.

Aside from looking at your college or university's own compliance efforts, what can you do that will set you on the right track? The discussion above about finding coursework for those in the work world also applies for students. A background in law and in the various risk areas will be helpful. A good, solid business education is also relevant for this area. Any courses that add to basic management skills—public speaking, effective writing, project management, etc.—will stand you in good stead as well.[6] Understanding adult education is also a plus, because so much of compliance work involves training adults. Training in any of the specific risk areas is valuable too, although you want to be careful not to be overly narrow in defining your areas of interest. Ironically, too much good work in only one risk area can signal to potential employers that you are only a specialist in an area that does not interest them.

In your course work, look carefully for opportunities to do research and writing on compliance-related topics. There are quite a few topics in the compliance and ethics field that need further research and analysis. By picking the right topic, you could gain valuable knowledge that could help in the job search and in actual practice. A good research topic could provide a basis for networking with others in the compliance field. You could also develop it as a publishable piece, with input from others in the field.

You may wonder whether you should plan to enter this field directly upon graduation, or only years later after working in other parts of the business world. In the past, the advice would probably have been that no real opportunity to enter this field existed directly from school. For the most part, some experience is still generally required, but more opportunities for junior level people are arising as the field matures. To those who say such entry level work does not exist, the interview with Timken's Rodney Smith shows that, in fact, these opportunities are developing.[7]

Reading in this field

It has been said in other contexts that to get information you need to be able to give information as well. By the same token, in the compliance and ethics field you will bring more to the table if you have acquired useful knowledge about the field. Personal networking is one way to do this, but a substantial body of literature exists that can provide you with enormously valuable insight. While social contact with compliance practitioners certainly increases your visibility, you can further augment your perceived value by being a source of useful information and ideas, much of which you can get simply by paying attention to the relevant literature.

A practical starting point can be the Integrity Interactive primer mentioned earlier, *A Guide to the World of Corporate Ethics and Compliance Programs*. This tool covers what should be in a typical compliance program, provides a chronology of the history of the field, and explains the terms and acronyms commonly used. It also includes a list of potential compliance risks and a brief explanation of possible privileges applicable to compliance work. The primer can serve you as a handy reference.

For a regular flow of interesting and practical ideas, subscribe to *ethikos*, a bi-monthly publication (Joe Murphy is an *ethikos* editor and owner). There you can find interesting tips and hear about how companies are approaching different compliance challenges. Another source for compliance news is the BNA publication *Prevention of Corporate Liability Current Report*. This monthly publication can keep you current on developments, especially those with legal implications. You can also join the Society of Corporate Compliance & Ethics and receive their useful magazine, *Compliance & Ethics*.

If you have a big appetite for reading, then consider tackling the book *Compliance Programs and the Corporate Sentencing Guidelines*, published by West and edited by Jeff Kaplan, Joe Murphy and Win Swenson. This annually updated text offers detailed coverage on developing and implementing an effective compliance and ethics program, a useful resource for those with that responsibility, whether new to the job or a veteran. You will find other sources to consider in Appendix C, "Where Can I Get More Information and Advice?"

But not all your reading need be the specific "how to" of compliance. Some of the best insights can come from learning the horror stories of companies that failed to have the right compliance program. Such books also make interesting reading, even for those who are not compliance "junkies." Appendix D, "War Story Reading," will give you a real-world immersion into the stories of these failures.

Getting training

Self-teaching and networking can bring you valuable background for the compliance and ethics field, but you should also consider what formal training is available to help you succeed in this field. There are a number of possible sources for training outside of company compliance programs. Remembering that this field is not just *compliance*, but also *ethics*, you might consider taking courses on business ethics, either at the undergraduate or graduate level. This is a step to consider carefully, based on where you are interested in working. There is some controversy in this field surrounding the role of ethics, especially when associated with an academic approach. There are some who see ethics courses as important training for people in business, helping them to reason through to the right results in areas where the decisions are not dictated by law; others view the universities' coverage of this topic as unrealistic.

It is advisable to explore with people in the positions that interest you whether such coursework is an asset or an unnecessary expenditure. You should also find out in advance whether the courses are practical and case-oriented, or more theoretical and academic. In general, we would recommend some exposure to this area, but not as the primary focus of your training.

Another source to consider might be courses in law school, or law-related courses in business school, for there is certainly value in understanding the legal system if you are going to be involved in compliance. If you have found a particular compliance area that interests you, such as environment or privacy, then finding law courses in a select area will be a pragmatic addition to your resume. While having a legal background is not essential, it is a definite advantage and worth pursuing when and where it is available.

There is also training available specifically addressing the practical aspects of compliance and ethics. The Ethics & Compliance Officer Association, in conjunction with Bentley College, offers a week-long course at Bentley College outside of Boston on the "how-to" aspects of this field. The course, called Managing Ethics in Organizations, offers general background training that allows for immersion in the subject of compliance.

SCCE holds a major annual conference, a four-day intensive academy, and workshops around the country that are open to those with an interest in the field. Similarly, HCCA offers seminars for those in the health care industry, both nationally and through its chapters, as well as a four-day intensive academy.

The Practising Law Institute (PLI) runs two-day programs annually providing insight on legal developments affecting the field, but also includes how-to coverage. You do not need to be a lawyer to attend these programs. The Conference Board also has a two-day business ethics program each spring in New York City, which includes compliance-related topics.

One other aspect of training to consider is "specific risk-area" coverage. You might decide that the one area that interests you is environmental protection, or employee safety, or perhaps privacy, so in addition to learning the basics of compliance, you could then benefit from learning about your preferred risk area. In a field like environmental protection, this education could range rather far afield, including an understanding of the science involved. In safety, learning about human health would be helpful, while a career in privacy compliance would require an understanding of the technology used to retrieve, process and store sensitive personal data. To access such specialized training, talk with those in your specific risk area to learn which sources of training would be most effective and accessible for your circumstances.[8]

For more detailed information on the training available in compliance and ethics, see Chapter 9, "What Training and Certifications Are Available for Compliance Professionals?"

Skills and character

Before you get too far into the process of exploring the compliance and ethics field, you should make an honest assessment of your own characteristics. Develop a feel for how others perceive you, and as part of this assessment, conduct an inventory of your own strengths and weaknesses. Being successful in compliance does require certain personality traits and skills.

In terms of characteristics, the first should be obvious: You need to be upstanding and ethical in all areas of your life. You need to be the type of person who believes in doing what is right. To stand by that belief in the corporate context, you also need strength of character and courage. Compliance work can place moral and social demands on people—you may have to be the minority of one who opposes something everyone else thinks is necessary. This is no small order for someone concerned about his or her career. If you can get people who know you to be honest with you, it is especially useful to hear how they perceive you. Of course, if you are looking to move into a compliance function in your own organization, having a reputation as someone who is not honest and ethical can be lethal to your ambitions. But if you are known as a person of strong integrity, this in itself can help lead to your being brought into the compliance effort.

Assuming you have the character, you must next consider the skills needed in the compliance and ethics field. While strong character is a necessary starting point, you also need to understand that much of compliance work is political. That is not to say it involves underhanded wheeling and dealing; rather, this observation just acknowledges that things get done in organizations socially, and you need to know how to get results with people. Good social skills, for example, can help you get the attention of managers who control needed resources. These skills will also allow you to convince employees that your compliance and ethics message deserves their attention. Having a good political sense will mean you recognize the value of benchmarking and obtaining buy-in for ideas and documents (like the code of conduct) before launching them on unprepared audiences.

Another highly valuable skill is public speaking. Can you get up in front of a group, whether it is 5 or 250 people, and speak in a way that reaches them? Can you explain difficult concepts in an understandable way? Can you convince an audience that what you say is true? If this has not been your strength you should not despair; a surprising amount of good public speaking is learned behavior. You can pick up valuable pointers either from reading about the subject, or from a coach or mentor who knows those fine points. Seminars on this skill are also available. You should then look for opportunities to practice and develop these presentation skills. Find a sympathetic audience, and actually practice your presentations.

Related to this skill is the ability to run meetings and achieve results from them. Much of compliance requires teamwork and obtaining support from others. For example, one of the core elements of a compliance program is the compliance committee. Its members typically include managers from different parts of the business who will bring a mixture of perspectives to the process. A compliance manager needs to be able to bridge the gap between different perspectives and move those people ahead toward a common goal. The manager also needs to know how to avoid the risk of being bogged down in a bureaucratic morass.

Another important skill is the ability to sell. Those in compliance are always in the business of selling: first, selling management on the need to have a compliance program, and then, on a day-to-day basis, selling all levels of the business on the continuing importance and relevance of the compliance efforts.[9]

Writing is another core skill needed. A typical compliance program will often start with the creation of a code of conduct. Writing this document can be a difficult challenge, covering sometimes-complex areas of the law, but in a way that untrained employees can readily understand. Communicating by email, communicating through the Web, writing company newsletter articles, drafting policies—all of these activities demand effective writing skills.

In addition to these essential skills for leadership in compliance, other proficiencies are useful when moving into this field. As is probably true for most if not all management functions, computer abilities are a key asset. While it may be possible to rely on staff, it is much more practical to be up-to-date in the use of computers. Similarly, competence in using the Internet for research purposes is a good skill to have, enabling the compliance person to access valuable resources quickly and efficiently.

Depending on the nature of the company, foreign language skills can aid with compliance tasks. For global companies, the ability to relate closely with groups of employees helps convey the compliance message. A compliance person must have a way to effectively carry the compliance message to significant operations in China, France, Argentina, or wherever branches of the company exist. Of course, if the headquarters of the company is located in another country, language skills could be absolutely necessary.

Specialization in specific risk areas

For the most part, this discussion of compliance programs has focused on the generic program covering all the compliance risks. But there is an alternative path: devoting your attention to one specific risk area.[10]

How feasible is this sort of specialization? The answer depends on the risk area you select. Some involve highly legalistic areas that likely will require a lawyer—antitrust is one of the best examples. Because of the high risk of criminal implications for misconduct, and the technical aspects of some parts of the law (e.g., Robinson-Patman Act, monopolization), lawyers almost always need to be involved in compliance activities in antitrust. But compliance programs are not the exclusive domain of lawyers, and this point is also true for many of the risk areas. Some require technical expertise, while others are fairly general and do not need technical or scientific expertise. Such non-technical areas are certainly open to the business generalist who is interested in doing compliance work in that specific field.

Some compliance risks deal with areas that are industry-specific. For example, the pharmaceutical industry devotes a great deal of attention to compliance with FDA requirements; those in aviation need to assure compliance with FAA standards. Likewise, in the health care field, compliance people need to have extensive expertise in dealing with Medicare/Medicaid.

In these technical areas, being an expert on the subject can prove even more valuable than having a legal background. In areas like workplace safety, Federal Acquisitions Regulations, export control and Medicaid/Medicare, lawyers will often step back and let the technical person handle the bulk of the compliance work. The lawyers are then only called in for novel legal questions.

Some risk areas are technical, but apply across a broader range of the economy. One of the best examples is environmental compliance. Any company that can affect the water, air or land needs access to environmental compliance expertise. Professionals in this field will find a background in the sciences that deal with pollution to be essential. The frustrated chemistry major who finds his or her talents wasted in a headquarters staff job might find this an appealing area to explore. Environmental compliance also has appeal because it is an area where the objectives are visible; one can see the results of pollution, whereas other risk areas (antitrust, Medicare/Medicaid, government contracting) are not so visible.

For those without a technical or legal background, there are compliance areas that reach beyond just one particular industry. Equal employment opportunity and privacy fall into this category. A person with no technical or legal expertise could decide that discrimination or privacy involves policies and issues that are personally important to him or her, and therefore worthy of pursuit. Whatever specialty you select, ask those in the field about organizations, training programs and publications that cater to that specific area.

While going into compliance at the general level means developing a skill that is very mobile, focusing on a specialized area can be limiting and even precarious. If you become identified with a specific risk area you may well be pigeonholed and excluded from consideration for other positions outside of that narrow zone. The message here is that if you select an area, be sure that is what you want. If your choice is too narrow, you may find you have limited your career options for the future.

Writing in this field

Assume you have made up your mind that you want to enter this field and be successful, to make your mark. If you are also the type of person who is comfortable expressing yourself in writing, you should consider writing about subjects in this field. For someone who is not already experienced in compliance, research and writing can be a good way to learn more while developing important credentials.

One reason that writing is a viable avenue for advancement is that the field of compliance and ethics is still relatively new, continually in development and open to new ideas and perspectives. While there have been more laws and government guidelines created recently, these still leave ample room for interpretation. There are new trends and developments waiting to be examined. This is also a field where some basic questions have not been satisfactorily answered. For example, there continues to be spirited debate over how to measure the effectiveness of compliance efforts. There is also surprisingly little literature providing specific guidance on such a fundamental point as how to conduct compliance audits. There are also numerous examples of creative initiatives in companies waiting to be discussed.

Where can you get your material published? The number of outlets is not yet large. Since author Joe Murphy is co-editor of *ethikos,* a bi-monthly journal covering practical approaches to compliance and business ethics, he can recommend this publication. Even with contributors who regularly scout out the field and provide materials, *ethikos* is always looking for useful material from good writers. Practical examples from the field are especially appreciated. Publishing an article in *ethikos* says much about a person's interest in and familiarity with the field.

Lawyers will want to consider the numerous law reviews as well as the bar press. These are not as practical in approach, tending to focus more on case law developments, but even a legal piece can send the same message that the author is someone to be considered in this field.

One of the benefits of writing a practical piece is that your writing project can serve as a good basis for valuable networking in the field. For instance, if your focus is a particular practice in compliance programs you could contact those who work in that area, reviewing the agendas of the ECOA, SCCE, PLI, and other programs to see who shares that interest. After making contact with the experts, you could compare ideas and request reviews of your draft articles. Conducting surveys is another way of pursuing networking. While you should not count on the people you contact offering you a job, the more you network, the greater the likelihood that you will hear about opportunities. If through your writing you do become identified with certain areas of compliance, it is more likely that others will think of you when issues come up in that area. Successful publication can also lead to invitations to participate in some of the programs put on by organizations like PLI, SCCE and ECOA.

One other writing strategy to consider is finding a good co-author who is already established. If you develop ideas for publication in your area of interest, you may find others already established in that area who would be willing to work jointly with you; they may even have had similar ideas but lacked the time to pursue them. As the junior member of the writing team, you would likely be expected to put in the bulk of the time and research, but your partner would help you gain acceptance and recognition. The authors of this book have employed a similar arrangement themselves.

Selling the program if there is none in an organization

One additional strategy that may be available to you is selling the idea of a compliance program to a company, university or other organization that does not have one. Even today, after years of development in compliance and ethics, some companies, and some entire parts of the economy, do not have compliance programs. Still others have very little that would meet the Sentencing Guidelines or other standards. Those with programs may have overlooked or underestimated entire risk areas.

Where are you likely to encounter this opportunity? Much of industry—at least the larger companies—has already accepted the need for compliance efforts, but there are entire areas of the economy that have not. For example, as ironic and even humorous as it may seem, the very law firms that are telling companies how to develop their compliance programs rarely have one themselves. Consulting firms, again including those who give advice in this area, similarly may ignore their own vulnerability. Somewhat less surprising, nonprofits, unions, and the non-medical side of universities often have done nothing, although some universities have recently begun embracing the need. For students and others interested in prodding their universities to action, the University of Texas has been leading the way in this proselytizing effort.[11]

Even in companies and other organizations that have begun establishing ethics and compliance programs, there may well be a need for someone to propose a more effective program. Perhaps there had once been a program that has suffered from neglect, or headquarters may have a program, but particular business units may be lax. Company joint ventures may also have been overlooked as areas deserving of compliance and ethics attention.

If you personally are recognized as conscientious enough to push this issue, your chances for being asked to assist in the program will certainly increase. Moreover, just the effort to sell the program will give you valuable experience and insight into the compliance and ethics world.[12]

Appendix 3A

Resume Builders: Things You Can Do to Advance in the Compliance and Ethics Field

Here are some insiders' pointers on how to build a strong resume to succeed in the compliance and ethics field.

1. Join the professional associations in this field: SCCE, ECOA, HCCA (for health care), ACI (Australia), etc. These are important sources for networking and information.

2. Join an industry or regional compliance forum. These are much more informal, and will introduce you to the key players in your industry or region.

3. Learn about a compliance risk area, e.g., privacy, environmental, antitrust, etc.

4. Work as a prosecutor or regulator. The experience in the "other camp" builds credibility.

5. Learn and master public speaking and adult learning techniques. This is a "how to" area—it can make all the difference.

6. Write and publish in the field—the more practical your approach, the better.

7. Hit the lecture circuit, once you are a good speaker and have a practical topic. Being a speaker on a compliance topic makes you an "expert."

8. Get certified where that option exists—e.g., SCCE's Certified Compliance and Ethics Professional (CCEP), HCCA's health care compliance certification, the UK's Compliance Institute, CFE's in fraud investigations.

9. Get relevant training, e.g., in compliance related skills or risk areas, such as law, audit, risk management, investigations, privacy, etc. MEO training helps in general compliance/ethics.

10. Get job experience in related areas, e.g., auditing, investigations, training course development, etc.

Endnotes

1. See Appendix C: "Where Can I Get More Information and Advice?" Another useful source is: Joseph E. Murphy, *Compliance Primer, A Guide to the World of Corporate Ethics and Compliance Programs* (Waltham, Mass.: Integrity Interactive, 2005). This booklet explains terms used in the field, gives you the history of corporate compliance programs, and provides background on what the field is about. The glossary and list of acronyms from the *Primer* are included in this document as Appendix A.

2. See Chapter 9: "What Training and Certifications are Available for Compliance Professionals?"

3. See Appendix B: "Sentencing Guidelines Definition."

4. The one difficulty with the ECOA, however, is that only those who are already inside doing this work are allowed to be members, thus limiting the networking opportunities for those seeking to enter the field. However, you can still gain some preliminary information by visiting this group's Website.

5. See Joseph E. Murphy, "Compliance Programs for Universities: Are the Risks Being Addressed?" *ethikos* 13, no. 2 (Sept/Oct 1999).

6. Refer to the compliance and ethics model course curriculum in Chapter 9: "What Training and Certifications Are Available for Compliance Professionals?" when trying to identify course offerings.

7. See Chapter 8, interview of Rodney Smith.

8. In privacy, the field has grown so explosively in the past few years that we have devoted a separate chapter to that topic; see Chapter 7: "Compliance Work in the Field of Privacy and Data Protection."

9. For more on this topic, see Chapter 10: "Selling Compliance (and the Importance of Your Job) to Management."

10. One list of such risks is set forth in Chapter 1: "What is This Field?"

11. See Joseph E. Murphy, "Effective Compliance Systems in Higher Education," *ethikos* 18, no. 1 (July/Aug 2004); and David B. Crawford, Charles G. Chaffin and Scott Scarborough, *Effective Compliance Systems: A Practical Guide for Educational Institutions* (Altamonte Springs, Fla.: Institute of Internal Auditors Research Foundation, 2001).

12. For more advice on how to sell a compliance program to an organization, see Chapter 10: "Selling Compliance (and the Importance of Your Job) to Management."

4 What Are the Jobs in Compliance/Ethics?

For those who read in the news that "compliance officer" is now a "hot job," they might think that there is just one opportunity per company. In fact, there are a great number of positions and titles in the business world that involve full- or part-time compliance and business ethics work. We are providing here a survey of positions that play a role in the compliance and ethics field. The first category covers those that are inside companies and other organizations. The second category includes those who provide compliance and ethics related services from outside. It also includes providers who offer training and other services to practitioners in this field.

In Appendix 4A, we have provided examples of a few titles and positions we have seen in this field.

Within Organizations

Chief compliance officers—Chief compliance officers are usually at the executive level, one per company. Some are full time, but most have other responsibilities. In the United States this position is typically intended to meet the Sentencing Guidelines standard calling for companies to have someone "within high-level personnel . . . assigned overall responsibility for the compliance and ethics program."[1]

Ethics officers—Sometimes this term has the same meaning as compliance officer, but in a few companies there may be separate structures for compliance and ethics. The ethics officer role may be limited to a few functions like handling the helpline and administering the code of conduct, but not dealing with the subject matter risk areas like antitrust or overseas bribery.

Assistant compliance officers—In some compliance structures, and especially where the compliance officer is not full time, there may be an assistant officer with day-to-day responsibilities for the compliance office. This person would typically be high level, but not an officer position.

Business unit compliance officers—As companies develop their compliance programs they realize that to reach the subsidiaries and other business units it is necessary to have managers in the business units who share the compliance mission. These are typically officers or high-level managers in the business units. They may have dual reporting relationships to the business unit management and the headquarters compliance office.

Business unit compliance directors/coordinators—This is a position at the next level below the business unit compliance officer. The compliance program may have coordinators or other representatives throughout the business. For example, each plant might have an environmental coordinator; each sales office might have a compliance director. This position may have a dual reporting relationship, both to management within the business unit and to a headquarters compliance counterpart.

Compliance staff—In larger companies there may be a separate unit devoted to compliance matters. These positions may answer in-house helplines, arrange training, assist in coordinating meetings, work on reports for management, monitor investigations, etc. They may range from senior positions to clerical posts. Staff may include specifically "compliance analysts," a role described below, under "Outside of Organizations." For individuals without prior business or compliance experience, this position may be one of the most accessible.[2]

Internal audit—The internal audit organization is often a participant in company compliance programs. There may be auditors or an audit unit specifically dedicated to compliance reviews. A senior person in internal audit will often be a key member of a company's compliance committee. Auditors also will participate in compliance investigations involving accounting and financial matters.

Compliance lawyers and paralegals—Many in-house lawyers play leading roles in company compliance programs. In some companies a specific lawyer may be designated as the compliance officer's or compliance program's counsel. Other lawyers may be the subject matter experts for risk areas such as antitrust, environment, or EEO. Legal assistants and paralegals in company law departments may play an important role in managing and assisting in compliance program functions. In some companies the general counsel may also have the compliance officer title, although this is somewhat controversial.[3]

Security—Depending on the industry and company, the security organization may have an important place in the compliance picture. In the telecommunications industry, for example, security participates in sophisticated investigations covering such allegations as fraud. Security people at larger companies may have law enforcement backgrounds, such as FBI experience, and may be Certified Fraud Examiners.

Corporate secretaries—Corporate secretaries are responsible for communications with and treatment of the board. As corporate governance structures continue to evolve, many have started to take on more of a compliance-related role. For example, they may play a role in arranging appropriate compliance training for the board.

Human resources—HR typically covers many issues and activities that are squarely in the compliance camp. HR managers would usually be responsible for EEO, harassment, wage and hour issues, immigration, FMLA, etc. They would also be key players in such compliance-related functions as discipline, evaluations, training and background checking. For companies with compliance committees, HR is an essential participant.

Inspectors general—In government agencies these positions have compliance-related responsibilities involving detection of wrongdoing. They function in an internal policing role.

Environmental engineers/experts—Environmental compliance matters in industrial companies are often handled by environmental specialists.

Risk management—Risk management departments assess risks, including compliance risks, facing the organization. While much of this analysis deals with non-compliance related business and environmental risks, their work also includes legal and reputational risk.

Ombuds—These are very specialized positions, and often have a role limited to acting as neutral intermediaries. The ombudspersons are available for employees to raise ethical and compliance concerns within the company but outside of the usual management chain of command. There is debate in the ombuds community about whether ombuds should ever conduct investigations, or take a more activist role. Their role is to counsel the employee on what steps to take next; from a compliance perspective; they help the company bring to the surface issues that might not otherwise be reported by employees.

Privacy officers and staff—This is a specialized area of compliance, but with requirements similar to other compliance areas. In some companies responsibility for the privacy function is assigned to the compliance officer; in others it is a stand-alone position. In the health care field this position may specifically include HIPAA compliance. In addition to the privacy officer, or in place of an actual officer, there may be more junior or supporting personnel.[4]

Governance officer—There was a time when corporate governance seemed to be a sleepy backwater of the corporate world. But after the Enron era and the passage of Sarbanes-Oxley, this area has become highly visible. While it does deal with issues that are usually separate from compliance, such as executive compensation, it also has taken on more of a compliance and ethics orientation.

Sarbanes-Oxley compliance manager—Sarbanes-Oxley did not just affect the lives of compliance and ethics people; it has even created its own field. Even companies that have had established compliance programs have at least temporarily engrafted onto the corporate structure managers or even departments to ensure compliance with Sarbanes-Oxley.

Corporate responsibility officer—Compliance and ethics as a field includes more than just obeying the law; it also includes values and ethics. A field that is at least related to the values side of compliance and ethics is corporate responsibility. While its focus may include obeying society's rules, it also tends to encompass areas such as aiding communities and protecting "stakeholders" beyond the shareholders. To some, this position is considered a form of public relations, but to others it is the natural extension of compliance and ethics. Larger, more publicly visible companies may have separate officers or even small staff groups that manage this area.

Regulatory affairs—In highly regulated industries, companies may have organizations devoted to the regulatory requirements. Examples would include telecommunications and energy. These people often play a liaison role with the regulators.

Government contracting specialists—In companies that deal with the federal government there may be entire units devoted to assuring compliance with government contracting requirements.

Outside of Organizations

General practice law firms—Lawyers in these firms may specialize in particular areas of compliance; a few lawyers focus on compliance as a specific topic. The most reputable firms are often called upon to conduct or at least assist in sensitive investigations of corporate wrongdoing.

Compliance specialist law firms—Lawyers in these firms limit their practice to the compliance and business ethics field.[5]

Accounting firms—The Big 4 firms provide advice to companies regarding their compliance programs and may also conduct reviews, audits or assessments of compliance programs.

Expert witnesses—As company compliance and ethics programs play an increasingly important role in litigation and government investigations, there will be a growing need for experts who can provide advice and testify about the bona fides of company programs.

Professors—Universities offer courses in business ethics, both for undergraduates and graduate students. In a few instances compliance is taught in law schools.[6] This area is one where it would still be necessary for anyone interested in the field to play the role of trailblazer, convincing schools that compliance and ethics topics should be taught. See Chapter 8, interview of Richard Gruner, for an example of one law professor's experiences.

Ethics/compliance consultants—These service providers offer advice on compliance and ethics programs. At least in the United States, if they are not lawyers they may not provide legal advice regarding compliance with legal standards. Some may specialize with particular strength in areas such as communications.

Compliance analysts—These are management-level positions in consulting and law firms that specialize in compliance work. This is one potential entry point for those interested in the field. One would expect the initial work to be heavy in research, but this does provide a useful learning opportunity.

Ethics institutes/centers—There are a substantial number of these centers in the academic world. The larger ones have staffs who work in the business ethics field, but most are relatively small with little or no opportunity for employment. For more information, see Appendix E.

Compliance/ethics publications—There are a number of ethics and compliance publications, but these tend to be relatively small. These employ editors and writers knowledgeable in this field. You will find several such resources listed in Appendix C, "Where Can I Get More Information and Advice?"

Helpline/hotline providers—These companies typically offer to handle helpline/hotline calls that companies receive. Jobs in these companies range from answering the phones to setting up data management systems that monitor helpline cases. They may also include communications positions to help customers publicize their helplines to employees.

Investigation firms—These companies provide services to companies that outsource their investigations. Such outsourcing typically occurs for the more complicated cases.

Online training providers—turn-key services—Training providers can offer companies and other organizations compliance training courses on an online basis. Jobs in these companies range from course writing, to technical experts, to sales and account management. This area has been one of the fastest growing in the field.

Online training contractors—Contractors work with companies that want to create their own, specialized computer-based training.

Compliance video providers and producers—These companies provide ready-made videotapes on compliance risk areas. Some providers specialize in areas such as HR compliance and workplace safety. Others work with companies to produce training videos. Typically the companies would provide the content and the provider would bring the production expertise.

Compliance software providers—Software providers offer companies software and information systems that assist in various compliance functions. These companies have become increasingly popular among corporations and organizations responding to the requirements of Sarbanes-Oxley section 404. Estimates were that in 2005 compliance spending on technology would reach $7.5 *billion* dollars and grow 22 percent annually. Compliance has become one of the highest-growth markets in technology.[7]

Ethics/compliance associations—Organizations such as the ECOA, SCCE, HCCA, and ACI offer member companies and individuals a range of services such as symposia, networking, and libraries of reference materials. These organizations include the managers and the staff who deal directly with members in providing services; many of these individuals are experienced veterans having worked previously in other areas of the field. The staffs also include those with skills in arranging and organizing membership meetings. Employment in these organizations can be an entry point to other parts of the field, as well as a follow-up career after working in-house.

Crisis response firms—There are firms that provide services to companies faced with crises such as government investigations and environmental disasters. These firms also offer advice on how to avoid such disasters.

Background checking firms—When hiring, promoting or transferring employees, companies turn to outside firms to check the backgrounds of the employees, especially for prior conviction records.

Employment/search firms—When compliance people are looking to change employers, or companies are seeking outside talent for their compliance positions, they turn to these providers.

Monitors—If a company gets in trouble with the government and wants to come clean, it may convince the government to defer prosecution and allow the company to clean up its house. But the price for this route may be an agreement that requires a monitor be appointed to check on what the company is doing. This outside provider would need to be acceptable to the government. Typically these are very prominent, experienced people, often with some government background. They are not employees of the company, although the company is required to pay for their services and expenses. For example, in order to avoid a prosecution such as the one that felled Arthur Andersen, in August of 2005 KPMG settled with the Justice Department over allegations of providing improper tax shelters, and accepted as a monitor former SEC chairman Richard Breeden.

Appendix 4A

What's in a Name:
Titles and Positions in the Compliance and Ethics Field

People who practice in companies and other organizations in the Compliance and Ethics field go by many titles and position descriptions. In our research, we compiled a list of over 800 distinct titles and positions. That list can be found in our larger book, *Working for Integrity: Finding the Perfect Job in the Rapidly Growing Compliance and Ethics Field.* Here, we have included twenty-five examples of positions in the field, both senior and junior level.

1. Assistant Ethics & Compliance Officer
2. Business Conduct Program Associate
3. Call Center Compliance Agent
4. Chief Compliance Officer
5. Compliance Analyst
6. Compliance Auditor/Trainer
7. Compliance Intern
8. Compliance Monitoring Assistant
9. Compliance Support Engineer
10. Corporate Compliance Paralegal
11. Counsel, Compliance
12. Director, Sarbanes-Oxley
13. Environmental Compliance Specialist
14. Ethics Assistant
15. Field Compliance Consultant
16. Junior Compliance Professional
17. Manager, Compliance/Ethics Training
18. Medication Compliance Researcher
19. Ombudsperson
20. Privacy Compliance Analyst
21. Regulatory Compliance Technician
22. Sarbanes-Oxley Lead/Compliance Associate
23. Senior Compliance Director
24. Vice President, Ethics
25. Web Compliance Reporting Analyst

Endnotes

1. This position is examined in more depth in Chapter 5: "The Top Job In-House: Compliance Officer."
2. For an example of an internal compliance analyst, see Chapter 8, interview of Rodney Smith.
3. For more detail on the compliance roles of lawyers, see Chapter 6: "Careers in Compliance for Lawyers."
4. Chapter 7: "Compliance Work in Privacy and Data Protection," explores this area of compliance work in more depth.
5. For an example, see Chapter 8, interview of Joseph Murphy.
6. See Paul E. McGreal, "Teaching Corporate Compliance: One Law School's Seminar Approach," *ethikos* 19, no. 1 (Jul/Aug 2005).
7. See William M. Bulkeley and Charles Forelle, "How Corporate Scandals Gave Tech Firms a New Business Line," *Wall St. Journal*, Dec. 9, 2005, A1.

5

The Top Job In-House: Compliance Officer

In the corporate world, the top position in compliance and ethics is the compliance or chief compliance officer. When positioned correctly, this person is a senior officer of the corporation, who would be elected by the board of directors. In some cases, however, the position may only report to the CEO or another officer, such as the general counsel. The position may be solely as compliance officer, or the title may be combined with another role, such as general counsel or CFO. The titles for this position can vary significantly. However, more important than the actual title is the issue of whether the position is truly a senior one with the necessary status and power to get the job done.

A compliance officer's objective is to ensure that the company establishes and maintains an effective compliance and integrity program. The officer ensures that the program is implemented as directed by the board of directors. There should be an appropriate information and reporting system so that the board and senior management hear directly from the compliance officer.

What is it like being a compliance or ethics officer? What does the job involve? We describe the job here based on some key job duties excerpted from a model position description (each major job duty is presented below in bold type). Working from those points we examine what the job really is, when executed effectively. The reader should note, however, that this discussion is not offered as a "how to" for establishing and running a compliance program. Such a guide would be much longer than this chapter.[1] Rather, our purpose is to provide insight into what the job entails, including some of the hurdles that can make the job a challenging one.

Exercise oversight responsibility for the corporation's global compliance and integrity program, reporting via unrestricted access to the CEO and board audit committee, if not the whole board.

The compliance officer is basically the manager who runs the show. One issue that commonly arises is the scope of the compliance program. Does it cover all compliance issues, or are some carved out? For example, the carve-out list might include some or all of these topics: privacy, environmental issues, health and safety, Sarbanes-Oxley, equal employment opportunity, and product quality (where it relates to compliance, such as in the pharmaceutical industry). The compliance officer may need to coordinate with others who have responsibility in these related areas, since no matter how the company divides up responsibilities, there will always be at least some overlap.

The compliance officer is the management position where "the buck stops." This officer deals with other officers, with the board, and with the compliance staff from all the business units. The responsibility for a global company should include operations in every part of the world.

The compliance officer is the compliance program's voice to senior management and the board. This person must be comfortable dealing face to face with the most powerful people in the corporate world. The effective reporting required of a compliance officer includes knowing exactly how to reach such busy people, and how to communicate in a way that has an appropriate impact. Where good communications channels have been established, the compliance officer should be very familiar to the top officers and the members of the board. The chair of the audit committee should be on a first name basis with this officer.

Part of a compliance officer's job is like that of any manager—to supervise those working in the program. In many organizations, however, this job duty may be more complex, because there will be compliance people within a company's organizational chart that do not have conventional reporting relationships to the chief compliance officer. In particular, the compliance officer may be sharing supervisory responsibilities with the line managers. Like other aspects of the compliance officer's job, this complication will require organizational skill in negotiating with these other managers on personnel issues.

Supervising in this field also has another element of difficulty—compliance people are different in certain key ways. While most employees need to learn to compromise and work as team members, compliance people also need to know how to do this without compromising on integrity issues. This detachment inevitably results in some pushback from other managers who think compliance people are not "team players" or are "difficult to deal with." A supervisor of compliance people, and especially the compliance officer, needs to be loyal to their subordinates in these key tests of strength. Yet, they also need to be alert to instances where the compliance staff may, indeed, be overzealous or antagonistic.

Because this give and take relates to compliance and ethics, the stakes can be very high, even when the disputes may otherwise seem relatively trivial.

The compliance officer should also make certain a system is in place to properly screen those working in the compliance program. This effort will obviously be done in conjunction with Human Resources.

Act as an advocate and champion of the compliance and integrity program among senior managers, and provide advice on compliance and ethics matters. Assist the senior managers in discharging their duty to ensure that the corporation has an effective compliance and integrity program.

The compliance officer will be the program's representative among senior management. The success and sometimes the protection of the compliance team will be in the hands of the compliance officer. He or she must be someone who is not intimidated by power and position. The compliance officer must be able to hold to unpopular decisions. But this determination requires more than just sticking a flag defiantly on the top of the hill. The compliance officer needs to earn the respect and trust of colleagues. The other officers must know that the compliance officer is prudent and practical, not placing unrealistic demands on the business, yet at the same time taking a no-nonsense approach to ethics and compliance with the law.

The compliance officer is also there for the senior managers as a coach and advisor. In the senior management meetings the compliance officer helps ensure that those making decisions are taking into account the code of conduct and the company's commitment to ethical actions. The chief executive, chief financial officer, and other senior officers should be able to turn to the compliance officer for advice on ethical and compliance issues.

In certain respects this responsibility is similar to the role played by the general counsel. Both will speak up when there is proposed illegal conduct. But the compliance officer has a broader responsibility, beyond the law. That duty includes focusing on what is ethical and consistent with the company's code of conduct. Another difference in the two jobs is that technically, the lawyer's role is to give legal advice, but not "run the business." Once that advice is given, it is up to management to decide how to proceed. The compliance officer has an obligation to act to prevent misconduct. This function is not just about giving advice; it is also about doing whatever is necessary to prevent the company from causing harm.

Ensure coordination with other company departments including the law department, internal audit, security, human resources, and information technologies to ensure effective implementation of the compliance and integrity program.

Being a compliance officer can never be a one-person show. It requires the ability to bring together managers and experts from every part of the business. Leadership in this context means not giving in to the temptation to try to do everything oneself. It means the ability to motivate others to pick up the banner of compliance and ethics.

Working with other key departments, often through committees established for this purpose, can bring added benefits, as it provides an opportunity to learn more about other areas of the business and to develop relationships with the business' leadership.

Someone considering a compliance officer job should have no illusions about the challenges of this position. In many companies, departments like legal and internal audit have well-deserved reputations for being strong players in the corporate organization. If not approached in an intelligent and well-thought out way, they can make the compliance officer's job extremely difficult. On the other hand, if the compliance officer is good in this function and can obtain buy-in by these key departments, this work can lay the groundwork for having a highly-effective program.

When a compliance project cannot be sufficiently dealt with internally, the compliance officer will also need to handle and supervise the retention of outside experts. External compliance perspective and tools may be needed especially in certain investigations, such as those involving senior officers.

Ensure that there is an effective system in place for employees and other agents to raise questions and obtain advice regarding compliance and integrity, and to report misconduct without fear of retaliation, and with appropriate follow-up.

One bedrock principle of compliance programs today is that there must be systems for employees and others to raise compliance questions. If an employee thinks his boss is cooking the books, or a sales agent thinks she is being asked to participate in illegal sales practices, each needs a way to raise these concerns or to obtain advice without first having to go to the person who is the cause of the concern. Thus companies today typically have helplines, increasingly supplemented with electronic reporting systems.

The compliance officer may have such a system staffed in-house, but it is common for companies to turn to professional service providers for this purpose. If a contractor is used, the compliance officer must ensure that the provider is responsive and professional in handling these often sensitive calls.

In addition to running a helpline, the compliance officer will also want to develop a system to keep his or her finger on the pulse of all such compliance inquiries and complaints. Typically only a fraction of these actually come in on the helpline. They also arise through other departments like legal, internal audit, HR, security and IT. The compliance officer needs to have a full view of all compliance-related developments. He or she also needs to coordinate these compliance-related activities, so that the left hand knows what the right hand is doing, and employees and managers do not feel that they are the random targets of constant compliance issues.

Of the various tasks that fall to the compliance officer, however, none is more challenging than the simple message of the Sentencing Guidelines: that employees and agents have a place to raise concerns without fear of retaliation. Preventing retaliation is a daunting challenge. Even with all the grand policy statements in the world, people may still shun whistleblowers, and angry bosses may still seek an opportunity to get even. Moreover, those who report misconduct may well have employment performance issues of their own. It falls to the compliance people to sort out these details, so that an employee whose performance has been marginal for some time is not suddenly found to be unacceptable immediately after calling in a complaint on the helpline.

Ensure that there is an effective and consistent system of discipline to address misconduct, and an evaluation and incentive system that promotes legal and ethical conduct.

Compliance people need to be involved in one of the most sensitive aspects of company life—punishments and rewards. When a violation is uncovered, the compliance officer needs to see to it that appropriate discipline is imposed. Moreover, because senior people represent the most risk and are looked to as models by the other employees, it is especially important that the disciplinary standards lean hardest on the most senior managers. Otherwise, you will have a situation best characterized as "the little fish fry while the big fish get away." Such an outcome will sour employees on the program, and can demoralize the compliance staff. To prevent it, a compliance officer must have a strong, innate sense of justice. Compliance officers also need to know how to bring other officers into the enforcement team, so that there is a broad base of support for discipline.

On the positive side, the compliance officer also needs to look at the rewards systems. The compliance program needs to have those who show leadership in compliance receive recognition and rewards. This system might require including commitment to the program as a part of all managers' personnel evaluations. Then, a compliance officer can provide very visible recognition for positive contributions by those in the compliance organization.

Ensure that there is a system in place for appropriate monitoring, auditing, and other measurements of the program's effectiveness and the corporation's compliance with law and ethical standards. The compliance officer should also ensure that all findings of misconduct and of weaknesses in the compliance and integrity program are responded to promptly and effectively.

The compliance officer needs to be someone who is not just comfortable with criticism, but who actively seeks it out. This job duty requires the ability to not take such input personally. For example, after each investigation the compliance staff needs to examine why and how the violation occurred. They will ask what was deficient in the compliance program that allowed the violation to occur. Their conclusions will include recommendations for improving the program. If the program is truly proactive this evaluation will be an ongoing process. No matter how good the compliance program and no matter how innovative, each time there is a violation and each time there is a review there will be findings that need to be addressed. The compliance program will be in a continuous improvement mode.

However, receiving the findings from the investigators or reviewers will not end the matter. The compliance officer then needs to see to it that the recommendations are in fact promptly responded to. Someone new to this process may at first be surprised that recommendations for improvements are not self-executing. Even when managers commit, in good faith, to adopt the recommended changes, there will nevertheless be frequent instances where not all the promises are kept. There will be additional priorities and emergencies for the managers, and in no time the promises may be forgotten and left unfulfilled. It thus rests with the compliance officer not only to seek out the criticism, but then to take on the role of monitor to ensure the fixes are actually implemented.

The compliance program needs systems to learn what is happening throughout the company, as well as to address all the significant compliance risk areas in the business. The compliance officer can work with internal audit to ensure that their reviews help with the compliance task. Similarly, the compliance officer will need to work with the law department to get assistance in planning a program of compliance reviews and their implementation. Programs need to review not only compliance with laws, but they also need to measure their own effectiveness. The Sentencing Guidelines standards require that an effective program include taking steps to prevent recurrence of the violation.

Ensure that appropriate records of the compliance and integrity program are generated and maintained.

The compliance officer always needs to have in mind the prospect of litigation and government investigations. After all, one of the purposes of a compliance program is to deal with the government and litigation. In any such circumstance the burden of proof is on the company to establish that it did, in fact, have a serious commitment to compliance. While the compliance officer and the staff can be expected to serve as witnesses for this purpose, simply having witnesses is not likely to be enough. The need to prove that the program is effective and meets the applicable legal standards will almost always occur in a difficult circumstance—when the government or an adversary can already prove that the company did something wrong. As the company's credibility is questioned, it will be critical for the company to have the ability to prove that its program was real.

In this context, a key responsibility of a compliance officer is to be sure that every element of the compliance program can be proven through documentation. At the same time, the compliance officer needs to be sure that the documents tell a positive story, and do not cause more damage to the company's position. Thus, for example, while it should be expected that every audit report and many investigation reports will show areas of weakness in the company's controls and compliance efforts, such irregularities may be acceptable if those same documents establish that the company promptly took steps to fix the weaknesses and enhance the program. The compliance officer, then, needs to assign someone the task of making sure that the program's records are in order and will stand the test of outside challenge. As with any department head, she will need to be sure that any legal requirements for retention of records are scrupulously followed for the compliance program's own records.

Keep current with compliance best practices and represent the corporation in external compliance and ethics forums.

The compliance officer will also be an external face for the company in explaining the company's compliance efforts and commitment. The officer and the compliance staff should be attending and participating in events and activities in the compliance and ethics field. This may involve speaking at conferences, teaching at universities, or being on leadership teams in compliance and ethics organizations. The compliance officer may sponsor formation of a local compliance practices forum, or play a role in coordinating an industry group.

It is essential that any compliance professional know what the trends are in compliance and ethics programs. Active involvement in compliance groups and organizations is a key part of this. There may also be opportunities for peer reviews and visits with counterparts at other companies.[2] One other, excellent way to perform this function is to be selected to serve on the boards of other companies. This effort gives the compliance officer an opportunity to observe first hand what another company is doing in its compliance program, while at the same time sharing experiences with that other company. (Because the compliance and ethics field has a strong tradition of sharing, this give and take poses little risk of improperly exposing confidential company information.)

Conclusion

It is clear that the compliance officer position calls for a collection of skills and expertise that is challenging. This review of compliance officer functions only offers an abridged look at what this job is like.[3]

Endnotes

1. See Jeffrey M. Kaplan, Joseph E. Murphy and Winthrop M. Swenson, *Compliance Programs and the Corporate Sentencing Guidelines* (Eagan, Minn.: Thompson/West Publishers; 1993 & annual supplement).

2. See David B. Crawford, "Using Peer Reviews To Assess Your Compliance Program," *ethikos* 18, no. 5 (Mar/Apr 2005).

3. For a more complete analysis, as well as several interviews with compliance officers, see Joseph E. Murphy and Joshua H. Leet, *Working for Integrity: Finding the Perfect Job in the Rapidly Growing Compliance and Ethics Field* (Minneapolis: Society of Corporate Compliance and Ethics, 2006).

6   Compliance Careers for Lawyers

Why would a lawyer want to go into the compliance and ethics field? Much of what a lawyer does involves coming in to fix things after someone else has created problems. This cleanup can be frustrating when you do it repeatedly. In compliance, the focus is to prevent bad things from even happening. Failing prevention, the task is to find the problems as early as possible and fix them to prevent people from getting into irreversible trouble. This set of tasks can offer a much more positive experience.

Compliance and ethics is also a developing field with new opportunities to make a difference. Certainly it is true that law can be dynamic and an engine of change. There is also no question that law is a well established field with set rules and processes in place. By contrast, there is more room for development and leadership in compliance and ethics because it is still so new.

Compliance and ethics work also offers an exit strategy for those who want something different from the traditional practice of law. This field offers the opportunity to cross into the business side, but without abandoning the positive elements related to law. It is an area where legal expertise is extremely valuable, but does not require the practice of law.[1]

How is compliance different from the practice of law?

Being in the compliance field differs in many ways from the conventional practice of law. In a sense, this newer field deals with the implementation of the law. The lawyer traditionally gives legal advice; the compliance person plays an active role in implementing this advice. The lawyer may advise a client not to do something; the compliance person's job is to see that the improper action does not occur. It is an activist mission.

Compliance and ethics work also goes beyond the legal realm to include values and ethics. One could discuss at length the theoretical aspects of this point, but the better way to summarize the point is that this field is about doing the right thing. It is important to understand the mission at this basic level, because compliance and ethics work must live in the world of the average employee. It is not about determining technical loopholes around the law; rather, it involves driving corporate cultures to support a mindset that seeks to do the right thing while still pushing ahead to business success.

This point also touches on another key difference between law and compliance. A lawyer has an ethical duty to represent the client zealously: "my client, right or wrong." It is then up to the legal system to sort out the truth. There is certainly a place for this approach in the larger scheme of things, but it is not the focus of the compliance person. Rather, the compliance person's duty to his or her client is more strongly tempered by a loyalty to the public and the profession.

There is also a difference in the nature of the work. As a compliance person you are not just the firefighter, called in when the house is burning to fight the flames. Your role is a preventive one as well. After the fire is extinguished, the compliance person needs to do the root cause analysis—sifting through the ashes to find the cause of the fire. Unlike the normal corporate mantra after a compliance disaster—"we want to put this behind us"—the compliance person wants the event to be viewed in detail, so that it can never happen again. This is not a perspective or skill taught in law school. But it is a central part of the Sentencing Guidelines standards (item 7 of the 7 standards)[2] and a core aspect of compliance work.

What are the advantages of being a lawyer for entering this field?

While there are various backgrounds that are valuable in the compliance field, lawyers tend to stand out as having many advantages for working in compliance and ethics. As a starting point, having knowledge and an understanding of the law is extremely useful in the compliance and ethics field. In some compliance areas it is close to essential to be a lawyer. For example, in antitrust or FCPA, it is necessary to understand the applicable laws. Of course, there is then a need to be able to explain legal principles in terms employees can understand. Ironically, in order to be able to make such complex areas simple and understandable, it takes a great deal of understanding of the fundamental principles in the particular area of the law.

In the past, much of compliance and business ethics practice was intuitive. But there has been movement over the years toward the adoption of legal standards. The best known of these is the Sentencing Guidelines, but legal standards for compliance programs have become more common with time. While the early standards were generally voluntary, there has been a recent trend to require either specific compliance program elements, or entire programs.[3] For better or worse, this change has tended to increase the role of lawyers. When the state of California requires an entire compliance program for pharmaceutical companies, the government of Canada requires privacy compliance elements, and the U.S. federal government mandates (through Sarbanes-Oxley) employee hotlines, it takes a lawyer to parse these legal standards to ensure compliance. In some cases, such as the American and French reactions to helplines, it can even call for reconciliation of conflicting legal standards. This trend toward the legalization of compliance standards could ensure that lawyers have an essential role in compliance for quite some time.

Lawyers tend to be analytical, and can focus on the facts to the exclusion of extraneous matters. This is drilled into lawyers in law school, and is part of the practice of law. Lawyers have to separate facts from emotions. Such critical analysis is an asset in compliance, especially in such functions as conducting investigations.

While the success of any compliance program requires engagement of employees and others, the fact remains that compliance must also deal with the risks of litigation and government investigations. Lawyers are familiar with litigation and the enforcement environment. This background is extremely valuable in compliance work. Lawyers are also well prepared for the crucial risk assessment process, which is needed in all compliance programs. Risk assessment can require an encyclopedic knowledge of the law to cover this task to the fullest extent. But even a lawyer without that level of background would still know how and where to start the process. In effect, a lawyer would realize how much there was to know, and assure that other lawyers were brought in to construct a fuller picture of the risks.

A lawyer would also be able to identify the legal risks of doing compliance work. This task is different from conducting a risk assessment of the company's exposure. Rather, the legal risks addressed here are those that accompany the compliance program's activities.[4] A lawyer would also be familiar with the law regarding privileges and confidentiality. This knowledge can become vital in compliance work when there is a need to keep material out of litigation so that it is not exploited against the company.

In short, lawyers have skills and knowledge that make them valuable participants in compliance programs. This fact is reflected in the high numbers of those with legal backgrounds involved in compliance work.

What are the potential disadvantages of being a lawyer in this field?

Being a lawyer has clear advantages when it comes to entering compliance, but the picture is not quite that simple. There are also some hurdles for lawyers. One of these is the risk of getting pulled into the great "ethics v. law," or "compliance v. values" debate. Ethics people may be concerned about being marginalized by the lawyers and legal standards. This can lead to debate and resistance to the inclusion of legal aspects of compliance. At times the nature of the debate can, unfortunately, remind one of the debate in *Gulliver's Travels* between those who believed eggs should only be broken at the big end, and those who believed that only the small end should be broken. It is useful to remember Jonathan Swift's message that wars can be fought over such disputes.

On the other hand, those who push for inclusion of values raise legitimate concerns about focusing overly on the literal language of the law. A lawyer needs to understand these concerns and learn how to appreciate the values focus. Lawyers also need to understand that the employees who aren't attorneys have a different sense of right and wrong, and what is ethical, that transcends legal issues. To an employee, mistreatment by a supervisor or extravagant compensation of an executive, while not illegal, will color that employee's sense of the company and its commitment to doing right. The wrong perception can open the door to truly illegal conduct. Without this more nuanced understanding, a lawyer could well be blind to this reality.

Another stumbling block for some lawyers is a litigation phobia that can cause them to elevate litigation over all other considerations. While everyone in compliance needs to be sensitive to litigation concerns, the primary focus must be to get the job done. Litigation risks need to be addressed, but should not be the foremost consideration. In the long term, the best way to address litigation risks is to do as good a job as possible in the compliance program.

Lawyers may also tend to be more reactive than proactive. Since lawyers are often called in after a problem has happened, they are around protecting their clients during dangerous moments. But when the danger passes the client typically moves on and leaves the lawyer to rush off to the next emergency. Effective compliance starts at the other end. While the emergency role is much more exciting, the compliance role in the long term can be more gratifying.

A lawyer conducting an internal investigation needs to be especially alert to legal ethics. It is always wise for a lawyer to explain to the interviewee in advance that the client is the corporation, not the individual, and that any disclosures the person makes are not protected. Only the company, not the individual, controls disclosure. If the interviewee asks if they should have a lawyer or asks to have a lawyer present, the company lawyer may then be in a difficult position and may feel compelled to stop the interview at that point. On the other hand, a non-lawyer conducting the interview for management (and not acting for a lawyer) has no such ethical compunctions. The non-lawyer could simply tell the employee (at least in the United States) either talk right now, or be fired.

A lawyer who is aware of the advantages of being a lawyer may not realize how much more a compliance person has to know than just the law. Of course, any person first coming into the compliance field may be surprised at the breadth of knowledge and experience required for compliance work. But because a lawyer already has background in the law, the temptation is stronger to assume one already knows what one needs to know. But in addition to legal expertise, compliance work calls for skills like project management, auditing, knowing how to train adults, and being able to communicate effectively. This requires a certain degree of humility, to recognize where legal background is not adequate and additional expertise is needed. It is one of the reasons that, no matter what the role of the lawyers in the program, it is crucial that managers from other parts of the business be brought into the program. Lawyers then need to be able to listen to managers with other areas of expertise.

How can you enter the field as a lawyer?

Weighing all the factors, you may decide that compliance and ethics is a field you would like to enter. How do you make the switch?

From law school

If you are in law school, the first step is to see if your law school has a course on this subject, or at least one that touches on this area. The South Texas College of Law has introduced a course specifically on this subject. At the University of Pennsylvania Law School, the course on Corporate Counseling includes specific coverage of compliance.

If there is no separate course on compliance at your school, then courses that may contain at least some coverage include corporate law, criminal law (if it includes white-collar crime), environmental, safety/OSHA, and employment law. But do not assume any of these include coverage of compliance and ethics topics; it is always wise to ask first. If you are at a university with a business school you could also check their curriculum for courses in such subjects as business ethics, but the same prior checking is needed to be sure that the courses cover relevant topics. If there is a business ethics course, scrutinize it carefully to be sure it is practical, and not theoretical, in its approach.

You can also consider looking for research opportunities in this area. This might involve writing a paper to meet a course requirement, or writing for a law review. Compliance and ethics is a good field for this work, partly because there are still many opportunities to make a positive contribution. Doing research can also provide a valuable opportunity to network with others in this field, which can be useful for future career prospects.

If applying to a law firm, you should ask the firm's attorneys if they handle this area for their clients. Of course, their natural tendency will be to say yes, so it is best to ask for names of specific lawyers who cover this area. You can then research their writing to see if they have, in fact, done anything on the subject.

Does it make sense going into this field right out of law school, versus pursuing other goals first? There are a number of options besides seeking to work in the compliance and ethics area directly out of school. You can work in enforcement, which is a very valuable background for a compliance person. You can pursue litigation experience. You can go into specific regulated fields with strong compliance elements, like employment law or environment, health and safety. Agencies like the EEOC, EPA and HHS OIG have published specific standards relating to compliance programs and have been actively focused on compliance efforts. If you are looking at joining a government agency, first inquire as to the agency's current approach and interest in corporate compliance work.

Another route is to first go into corporate work to get inside experience in a company. In compliance it is enormously helpful to understand how companies operate, and to be familiar with the politics of organizations. In-house experience also helps establish credibility with company management.

From a law firm

If you are already in a law firm, your field of specialty will have a major impact on your ability to move into compliance. If you do wills and estates or divorce counseling there is not much basis for making the move. On the other hand, if your specialty is already compliance, or a compliance-related area, then the transition becomes a matter of networking with potential employers.

If you would like to get real-world experience in compliance work, one available training route is possible, although it may well be painful. Simply try championing a compliance program in your own law firm. The likely resistance and skepticism you will receive will give you insight into what it is like in other companies initially, and still like in sectors of the economy that have not bought into compliance programs yet. (You will also begin to see why your clients do not quickly do all the things you recommend for the sake of their compliance programs—it is not easy to convince people, even lawyers, to do these things.) Although your effort in your own firm may not be successful, the experience will give you much better rapport with people in the corporate world who fight those battles daily.

From a company legal department

The transition from working in a company's legal department to working in its compliance and ethics department is certainly among the easiest to make. One approach is to focus on compliance in your risk area, including researching all the elements that apply in that area. Another route is to become familiar with all the legal aspects of compliance and become the company's resource for the legal side of compliance. Either or both steps would likely bring you into the orbit of the compliance program.

Know the key legal areas

For a lawyer, the route to becoming a compliance person involves mastering the legal standards that apply to compliance programs. Not that long ago there would have been very little to learn—there were no real standards and very little guidance. But that picture has changed dramatically. We are moving toward an environment where there are many sources of standards, guidance, and laws to be familiar with.

The first standard any lawyer needs to know is the Sentencing Guidelines. It is necessary to fully master the current version of the standards as revised in 2004. Of course, as with any legal standard it is also important to know the history, so a lawyer just coming into this field would also want to know the 1991 standards and how they were applied. There should also be familiarity with the "legislative history" of the 2004 Guidelines. This goal calls for review of the Report of the Ad Hoc Advisory Group on the Organizational Guidelines (Oct. 7, 2003). This lengthy report explains the background of the 2004 changes, and is the best source for understanding the purpose behind those changes. It also provides sources on other compliance standards.

While the Guidelines are the most important standards, they are not the only ones. There are a number of other legal standards applicable to compliance programs[5]. For example, in specific risk areas various regulatory and enforcement agencies have given their views on what should be in programs addressing their areas. The Office of Inspector General of the Department of Health and Human Services has issued lengthy guidelines on what should be in programs in various parts of the health care industry. EPA and EEOC have each issued specific guides on compliance efforts. Overseas there are a number of sources for guidance, including the Australian Standards (AS 3806), the Johannesburg Stock Exchange standards, and the provisions of the Italian anti-bribery statute.

A lawyer also should know the areas where compliance programs are no longer voluntary, but are required either by statute or stock exchange listing requirements.[6] For example, three states now require companies to provide training on sexual harassment. The state of California requires pharmaceutical companies to have compliance programs that follow the HHS OIG guidance for that industry. In the specific compliance area of privacy, both Germany and Canada make certain compliance program elements mandatory for companies, and in the United States, HIPAA requires privacy officers in the health care industry.

In the traditional way that lawyers approach case law, there have not yet been precedents interpreting the compliance standards of the Sentencing Guidelines. However, there are two areas that do shed some useful light. The first is the *Caremark case,*[7] which dealt with a set of facts regarding a compliance program that the Delaware Chancery Court commented on favorably. The larger, more detailed area of case law development is in the application of the U.S. Supreme Court's holdings in *Burlington Industries, Inc. v. Ellerth,* 524 U.S. 742 (1998), and *Kolstad v. American Dental Association,* 527 U.S. 526 (1999). In these cases the Court made it clear that compliance efforts are relevant in defending cases. In certain types of allegations of harassment such efforts might deflect liability; in the discrimination area in general they could be used to defend against punitive damages.

On the darker side of compliance, there is another valuable service a lawyer can provide that is almost the exclusive domain of the legal profession—advising managers on how to avoid the legal risks that can come with the very compliance activities whose purpose it is to prevent legal violations.[8] In this respect, the first job of the lawyer is to identify what these risks are. For example, it might never occur to a compliance trainer that students' notes could be used against the company in litigation, or to a code drafter that it could be an "unfair labor practice" to "impose" a code of conduct on unionized employees. With a firm understanding of these risks, the lawyer then needs to arrange useful guidance for the compliance managers—written guides, training, and readily available advice when needed.

Whatever your position in the legal field may be—law student, associate or partner in a law firm, regulator, or in-house counsel—doing this research will help enormously in making the transition. It will also serve as a check for you to determine whether this is the field for you. And, if you find some frustration from the absence of answers to your developing questions about this field, then you may also gain a deeper sense of how much opportunity there is for new ideas, research and analysis in compliance and ethics.

A paradox—lawyers who resist compliance

You might logically assume that lawyers will always be champions of compliance, and that any lawyer in a company will be sympathetic to the development of a rigorous compliance and ethics program. While many more lawyers today understand compliance than was true in 1991 when the Sentencing Guidelines were promulgated, there are still lawyers who do not like the whole compliance program idea.

For some lawyers, being a lawyer is about litigation, or doing other traditional aspects of legal practice. Deal lawyers want to get deals done, securities lawyers want to get the SEC filings done, and trial lawyers want to have control over discovery and trial work. For other lawyers, compliance programs are a diversion from real lawyering. For many, anything that interferes with litigation is unacceptable. It is as if litigation were an end in itself, rather than just one tool used by society to control misconduct and settle disputes.

Other lawyers resist compliance efforts because of an overwhelming fear of litigation. Anything that might possibly be used against the company in litigation, or be a basis for litigation, is viewed as totally out of bounds. They do not want serious compliance audits or publicity about disciplinary cases because they might lead to litigation—even though these are both compliance steps calculated to prevent harm and thus litigation.

Yet another objection by some lawyers is the idea of dealing with ethics as part of a compliance program. For these lawyers, they do not want to be the "conscience of the company," as one general counsel once stated. They give legal advice and it is up to management how to run the business.

None of these perspectives should deter a lawyer who wants to pursue compliance and ethics as a field, but they do serve as a warning. Compliance people simply cannot assume that all company lawyers will share their commitment. Lawyers who go into this field also need this awareness.

Conclusion

Compliance and ethics is not an easy field for anyone, including a lawyer. The work can be difficult and challenging, with resistance from many quarters, including fellow lawyers. But an effective compliance and ethics effort can be very positive and rewarding. This is a field where you can make a difference. You can help people and also help the field itself develop.

Many experienced lawyers can still remember the pre-law school optimism and faith in people that they brought into law school. Perhaps years of practice have deadened those sentiments. But if you are someone who still gets angry over abuses of power and still has a desire to make things better, a part of the business community will welcome your drive. Compliance and ethics is not for everyone, but it might be just the right path for you.

Endnotes

1. For a further discussion of the reasons why law may offer less satisfaction than the field of compliance and ethics, see Chapter 2: "Why Should I Go Into This Field?"
2. See Appendix B: "Sentencing Guidelines Definition."
3. See Joseph E. Murphy, "Mandavolent Compliance," *ethikos* 19, no. 2 (Sept/Oct 2005).
4. See Joseph E. Murphy, "Examining the Legal and Business Risks of Compliance Programs," *ethikos* 13, no. 4 (Jan/Feb. 2000).
5. A number of these sources are available through the SCCE Website, www.corporatecompliance.org.
6. See Joseph E. Murphy, "Mandavolent Compliance," *ethikos* 19, no. 2 (Sept/Oct 2005).
7. In re Caremark International Inc. Derivative Litigation, 698 A.2d 959 (Del. Ch. 1996)
8. See Joseph E. Murphy, "Examining the Legal and Business Risks of Compliance Programs," *ethikos* 13, no. 4 (Jan/Feb. 2000).

7   Compliance Work in Privacy and Data Protection[1]

Although we have devoted a separate chapter entirely to privacy, it is important to understand that privacy is not a separate field from corporate compliance as a whole. They are, in fact, interrelated. We have chosen to highlight this area separately because it is a large and rapidly growing sub-field of corporate compliance.

With advances in technology changing the way organizations do business and store and exchange personal data, privacy and data protection has become an important part of corporate compliance programs in a diverse set of industries. Now there are a myriad of privacy and security laws on the books, and companies are responsible for implementing a new series of policies and procedures aimed at meeting the requirements of the new legislation. These laws, coupled with the recent outbreak of high-profile privacy breaches among a few large organizations, stress the significance of companies maintaining privacy and security procedures as a part of their overall compliance system.

The importance of privacy programs

In February 2005, ChoicePoint Inc., one of the leading providers of consumer data services to insurance companies, businesses and government agencies, revealed that criminals posing as legitimate business associates gained access to their databases in late 2004, viewing the personal records of thousands of consumers. According to the Georgia-based firm, the thieves were able to acquire 145,000 records, resulting in one case of identity fraud. "Among the data available through the company's services, and possibly accessed by the criminals, are consumers' names, addresses, Social Security numbers and credit reports...."[2] After making this announcement, ChoicePoint Inc. released a report revealing a similar breach had occurred in 2000, prompting investigations by the Securities and Exchange Commission and the Federal Trade Commission.

ChoicePoint, however, was not alone. Shortly after their report was made public, a series of similar abuses began making headlines. Within a one-month period, Bank of America, T-Mobile, Science Applications International Corp., and Reed Elsevier Group's LexisNexis service all reported data theft and leaks. The sudden outbreak of privacy breaches captured the attention of the citizenry who worried that their personal information was ripe for the taking. High-ranking U.S. senators, such as Patrick Leahy of Vermont, called for hearings into how federal privacy laws could be drafted or amended to deal with these issues. In the meantime, pro-regulatory activists joined forces with private citizens in a bid to lobby Congress and the states for legislation aimed at regulating the collection and sale of data. Both groups want to prevent such information from being compromised in the future.

Whether regulatory requirements are imposed by Congress, or organizations are left to self-regulate, companies are now being charged with the task of improving the methods used to guard an individual's private information.

Companies alter their privacy policies

The more concerned the public gets about the safety of their private information, the more they demand that companies take steps to police themselves. For example, a Pew Internet and American Life survey found that 86 percent of respondents would like companies to develop "opt-in" policies and other procedures designed to regulate the disclosure of personal information.[3] Opt-in policies are those in which individuals, be they consumers or employees, are asked whether or not they want their personal information shared with any third parties. In response to this scrutiny, companies are taking steps to improve their privacy safeguards. The hope is that by implementing new procedures, companies will be able to avoid litigation, regulatory action, and the potential loss of customers. Violations can be costly in terms of fines, shareholder lawsuits, and even criminal prosecution.

To enhance the handling of private information, organizations are now creating positions whose sole task is to develop and monitor all in-house activities with privacy implications. Implementing procedures, however, is only one piece of the puzzle. Individuals must be in place to monitor whether or not these new procedures are achieving their desired effect. For example, periodic risk assessments will need to be performed to ascertain the probability of unauthorized access or disclosure of private data. This type of activity requires highly trained privacy professionals.

With privacy emerging as a major risk area for businesses, and with the creation of new positions to deal with this concern, privacy is fast becoming an area of employment that can provide a satisfying career that is in high demand. According to a study issued by the Ponemon Institute, most participating companies believe that privacy expenditures will increase over the next several years.[4] A fair amount of this spending is expected to be set aside for hiring and training.

Although organizations have been taking steps on their own to improve the ways in which they collect and store personal data, recent trends show that legislatures are starting to get more involved as well by passing comprehensive laws aimed at protecting the privacy rights of individuals. Typically these pieces of legislation will require a company to take appropriate steps to secure the protection of their stored information. These steps will be both technical and organizational.

Key Legislative Developments

Over the past few years, a variety of legislation has been passed both in the United States and abroad in an attempt to improve the methods used by companies to protect personal data. Although the U.S. government, along with governmental bodies at the state level, is beginning to place a great deal of importance on privacy regulations, the United States has typically followed a "hands-off" approach to data protection, relying heavily on an organization's decision to self-regulate. When the United States does draft privacy-related legislation, it tends to be narrowly tailored to address specific business sectors, such as health care, as opposed to sweeping legislation that affects all public and private organizations that collect and store personal information. Contrary to this approach, foreign governments, such as the EU, Canada and Japan, have all passed comprehensive legislation protecting the personal information of both consumers and employees.[5]

With laws now on the books calling for increased security measures, coupled with the advances organizations have made on their own, companies around the globe are routinely hiring privacy professionals in order to comply with these new standards. In order to provide a better understanding of how things are developing in the United States, this next section will briefly describe a key development and its effects on the field: U.S. passage of federal privacy-law in the health care field.

HIPAA

In 1996, Congress passed the Health Insurance Portability & Accountability Act (HIPAA) (Public Law 104-191), also know as the Kennedy-Kassebaum bill. The goal of this legislation was to improve the efficiency and effectiveness of the health care system.

When drafting this piece of legislation, it became apparent to certain members of Congress that as health care providers increase their reliance on electronic methods for data exchange and storage, certain provisions need to be in place to protect this information. In response to this concern, HIPAA included "Administrative Simplification" provisions that required the Department of Health and Human Services to adopt national standards for electronic health care transactions. Following HIPAA's mandate, HHS published its final regulations in the form of the Privacy Rule in December 2000, which became effective on April 14, 2001. This action cemented into law the first national privacy standards that afforded all Americans basic protections when it comes to safeguarding their personal information.

With the Privacy Rule in place, organizations in the health care field are hiring a number of new employees who possess an understanding of HIPAA and its provisions. Covered entities are required to create internal policies and procedures that will bring them into compliance with the standards in the legislation, and new positions are being created almost daily. The promulgation of these standards has placed health care at the forefront of data protection developments in the United States, providing a number of opportunities for individuals interested in joining this field.

Privacy v. Security

When looking for a career in privacy, it is important to note that the field is typically separated into two seemingly analogous divisions: privacy and security. While at first these two areas may sound similar, they are in fact quite different in focus and responsibility.

Privacy officers, and those who work under their leadership, are concerned primarily with making sure an individual's personal information is kept secluded from the view of others, unless third parties are given express authorization to have access because of a legitimate business need or legal requirement. Their responsibilities cover the privacy of, and access to, consumer information in compliance with laws and regulations. For example, Chief Privacy Officers might find themselves in a position to determine whether or not consumer data should be sold to a third party. Their duty is to protect the interests of their customers and assure that the company's policies and the laws are followed.

A security officer, on the other hand, is not charged with dissuading a company from selling consumer data to a third party. It is not his or her job to determine whether or not such a transaction is permissible. A data security officer instead focuses on making sure that when information is passed to another party, it is done so in a safe and secure manner—integrity of the systems is a key objective for him or her.

Some companies are tempted to combine these responsibilities into one position or office, usually in the guise of a Privacy & Security Director. This individual is responsible for developing and promoting activities that create security awareness within an organization. The director also plays a key role in making recommendations covering all operational aspects of privacy protection. Although a few such positions exist, our research has shown that more often than not these two activities are kept separate.

Privacy Positions

A. *Chief Privacy Officer (CPO)*

As the highest-ranking privacy official, Chief Privacy Officers are the individuals who create and monitor the entire system of safeguards that are necessary to protect the personal data stored by their organization. While CPOs are not usually considered to be executive level positions (although some companies do in fact have it as such), they often report directly to the CEO. The further removed the CPO is from the head of the organization, the less credible the initiative appears, and the less attention it gets.

In addition to reporting to the CEO, many Chief Privacy Officers are expected to work hand-in-hand with the organization's Chief Compliance Officer. It is important for the Compliance Officer to be kept up to speed on all policies, procedures, investigations and programs that are initiated under the supervision of the Privacy Officer. If each compliance area—privacy, environmental, safety, antitrust, etc.,— goes its own way on an uncoordinated basis, the result can be dysfunctional and cause an employee backlash; thus, areas like privacy will be less effective if they operate in isolation from the overall compliance program.

Roles and Responsibilities

Although the day-to-day responsibilities of CPOs may vary depending on the specific company they work for and industry they are in, we have included here a brief list of some basic duties that are shared by all privacy officers across the spectrum. This list was put together from publicly available job postings and job descriptions. (Please note that this list is not comprehensive.)

- Performs periodic risk assessments and compliance monitoring.
- Assembles and oversees the privacy team.
- Collaborates with legal counsel, senior management, and the heads of each department in the company to ensure the organization maintains

the appropriate privacy and confidentiality practices and consent vehicles (i.e., authorization forms, information notices and materials reflecting current legal practices and requirements).

- Establishes, oversees, and may in fact deliver, the privacy training to all employees, staff, and agents of the company.
- Implements an internal complaint system and resolution process. When a complaint is filed, the CPO is required to investigate. If the complaint turns out to be true, the CPO must take the appropriate steps to amend any policies or procedures in the privacy policy to prevent another occurrence in the future.
- Remains up to date on applicable federal, state and international privacy laws.
- Ensures that all customers, clients, and employees of the organization understand their privacy rights.

Background and Education

When it comes to being hired as a Chief Privacy Officer, experience goes a long way. On average, companies looking to hire a privacy officer are interested in candidates with at least 5-10 years of experience in the field of data privacy (including analyzing and applying privacy and data security practices). Ideally candidates for the position will also have some level of experience working in the industry in which they are applying, although a strong background in privacy, or prior experience as a CPO, will help make up for any lack of industry experience. Most important, however, a candidate for the position must understand the current state, federal and international legal and regulatory climate, along with how it impacts a company's business dealings.

Virtually every job description we reviewed for this position required applicants to possess a bachelor's degree, though not in a specific field. Although the postings require only a BA, preference is given to candidates who possess an MBA, and added preference is given to those with a law degree. In addition to experience and education, it is important for candidates to possess a few other characteristics that will help make them a more successful supervisor and CPO.

Privacy officers must be proactive. They have to constantly seek out the latest developments in their field and be able to incorporate these new techniques into their company's policy. Candidates must also possess a demonstrated ability to define the strategy of, and provide overall direction to, a specified practice area. You must also have excellent communication and writing skills, strong organizational skills, and an ability to exercise the highest ethical standards, professional demeanor and prudent business decision making despite pressing deadlines.

Salary

Although the salary for a privacy officer is not among the top five of a public company, "CPOs typically earn an enviable salary, well into six figures."[6] While this fact may vary depending upon the size of the company and the experience of the candidate, we found from reviewing online postings that the typical salary range for a *new* CPO is between $80,000 and $100,000.

In August 2005, the International Association of Privacy Professionals (IAPP) and Ponemon Institute published their third joint salary survey. As part of the survey, researchers asked a sampling of privacy professionals how much money they made per year in order to calculate the mean yearly salary for individuals in each position. According to their research, the average yearly salary for a Chief Privacy Officer is $157,055.

B. Privacy Specialist/Analyst

Once an organization's Chief Privacy Officer has drafted a set of privacy standards, personnel must be hired, and trained, to implement those standards. These individuals are commonly referred to as privacy specialists or privacy analysts.

Roles and Responsibilities

A privacy specialist is one member of an organization's privacy department. Typically an organization's privacy team will consist of one Chief Privacy Officer and one or more privacy specialists. The total number of employees will vary based upon the organization's size and needs. The privacy specialists report directly to the Chief Privacy Officer. Privacy specialists support implementation of the company's privacy strategy by performing various reviews to assess compliance with laws, regulations and internal privacy policies. They also work with management to identify any areas impacted by privacy-related laws and regulations. If they come to the conclusion that an incident has occurred, privacy specialists will assist in any remedial steps to be taken.

As with the Chief Privacy Officer, the day-to-day responsibilities of a privacy specialist will vary from one business to another. However, here is a brief list of the position's primary responsibilities:

- Maintain compliance and self-assessment documentation for new privacy and information security laws and regulations.
- Perform privacy compliance assessments by testing key privacy controls, systems and procedures.
- Assist in working with the Legal and Compliance departments to determine applicability and impact of current and pending privacy related legislation and regulations.

- Assist in working with management to identify functional business areas impacted and potential solutions for compliance.
- Assist in responding to actual or potential breaches of stored information on customers as well as employees.
- Assist in performing and maintaining documentation for annual privacy related risk assessments.
- Assist in development, review and execution of privacy training for employees.
- Maintain inventory of company privacy related training materials.

Privacy specialists assure that an organization's main line of defense against abuses is in place and working. They are ultimately responsible for the day-to-day maintenance and implementation of their company's privacy policy.

Background and Education

Companies looking to hire privacy specialists are interested in candidates with a bachelor's degree in a directly related field, e.g., business administration or information technology, with a minimum of three years of job related experience. Typically this experience will include one year in audit, compliance, information systems, legal, privacy, quality assurance or risk assessment. For those who might not have the requisite education, but have acquired the necessary experience, some companies will allow experience to replace education on a year-for-year basis. So, in this case, you would need at least seven years of experience in at least one of the areas listed above. Four of those years would make up for the absent BA, and the remaining three would cover the experience requirement.

Beyond the basic requirements of education and experience, you must also possess a few extra abilities that are deemed necessary for success in this position. For example, you must be able to communicate effectively, orally and in writing, in both meetings and presentations. You must have strong analytical and organizational skills and be able to apply these skills in a fast-paced environment. Typically this type of position requires you to be proficient in Microsoft Windows, with an intermediate level of proficiency in word processing (Word), spreadsheets (Excel), and Internet research.

Salary

According to the 2003 Privacy Professional Salary Survey Report, the mean yearly salary for a privacy specialist is $59,000.[7] If you are new to the field, there is strong likelihood that your initial salary will start around $40,000, depending upon your background and experience.

Transferring to a Career in Privacy from Another Field of Compliance

Prior experience in the field of corporate compliance, in any department within an organization, will work to your advantage when seeking employment in the privacy field. As noted earlier, companies hiring privacy specialists typically look for candidates with some experience in compliance, auditing, or risk assessment. Although the knowledge and experience you have acquired in these areas will be helpful, you will still be expected to have an understanding of the privacy concepts discussed above, including the various pieces of legislation that govern the field.

To make this transition, it is useful to understand that privacy is one piece of the larger compliance puzzle. When you are looking for employment in the field of privacy and data protection, and you are already employed as a part of your company's compliance structure, you are not moving to a department distinct from corporate compliance in general. You are simply shifting your focus from one aspect of compliance to another.

Training and Certification

In order to deepen your understanding of the legal, technical and business concepts that shape privacy and data protection, training and certification courses are offered for individuals looking to enter the field for the first time, or for those already employed who are looking to advance in their career. Having a series of training courses or professional certifications listed on your resume can help maximize your potential for success during an interview for a new job in privacy, or if you are seeking a promotion.

Most training and certification courses are offered to anyone who is interested in learning about the field, and who would like to obtain some type of documentation showing that he or she has acquired a professional understanding of privacy and its principles. However, there are instances where courses are set aside solely for Chief Privacy Officers and other high-level executives. In addition, training can be developed exclusively for lawyers as a way to help them better protect their clients from liability associated with the loss, destruction or misuse of personal information. Most certification exams do not require any training courses beforehand, however they do suggest that you enroll in a few to improve your chances of success in the test.

Training and certification courses focus on a wide range of topics, including:
- Privacy fundamentals
- Privacy and the law

- Workplace privacy
- Data sharing and transfer
- Web privacy and security
- The role of a CPO in the organization
- Governmental privacy

Conclusion

This review of privacy compliance and data protection offers a look at what this field is like, what types of careers exist, and what they entail. It is clear that the privacy positions outlined in this chapter call for a collection of skills and expertise that is challenging. Of course, these descriptions explain the typical requirements and qualifications necessary for success. Note that each employer's wants and desires will vary depending upon their organization's needs, its size, and the industry it is in.

Endnotes

1. This chapter was produced by Christopher Vigale, a former compliance analyst with Compliance Systems Legal Group.
2. See Matt Hines, "Scammers Access Data on 35,000 Californians," *CNET News.com*, February 15, 2005.
3. See John B. Horrigan, "New Internet Users: What They Do Online, What They Don't, and Implications for the 'Net's' Future," Pew Internet & American Life Project, 2004.
4. See Eric J. Sinrod, "Want privacy? Put your money where your mouth is," *USAToday.com*, March 31, 2004.
5. For more information on international legislation, see the expanded chapter on privacy in Joseph E. Murphy and Johsua H. Leet, *Working for Integrity: Finding the Perfect Job in the Rapidly Growing Compliance and Ethics Field* (Minneapolis: Society of Corporate Compliance and Ethics, 2006).
6. See Pamela Mendels, "The Rise of the Chief Privacy Officer: CPOs are a new breed of execs that combine tech and legal savvy—and the ability to say no," *BusinessWeek Online,* December 14, 2000.
7. See 2003 Privacy Professional Salary Survey Report, IAPP and the Ponemon Institute, February 2003. Note that, while IAPP and the Ponemon Institute conducted a more recent salary survey in 2005, they did not include information on Privacy Specialists in that report.

8   The Voices of Experience: Advice from Those in the Field

In this chapter, we have provided a handful of interviews with persons working in the field to serve as examples. The interviews were chosen from the 20+ interviews included in our longer book, *Working for Integrity: Finding the Perfect Job in the Rapidly Growing Compliance and Ethics Field*. The interviews provide examples of success and accounts of hurdles within the field, from those who are already established as compliance and ethics professionals. Moreover, the contributions made by the interviewees serve as evidence of the openness and integrity which characterizes the field.

Below we have listed the interviewees; along with each name, we have included a brief explanation for why we contacted them and what topics they are specially qualified to offer advice about.

It is important to note that the interviews contained in this chapter are reflective only of the personal opinions and experiences of the individuals interviewed. Interviewees are not included as representatives of any past or present employers, nor did their employers have any say in what has been printed.

These interviews are offered as a starting point; if you are interested in a career in compliance and ethics we encourage you to reach out for advice to people in the areas you think would most interest you.

Odell Guyton

We originally contacted Odell Guyton shortly after he assumed a high position with a major corporation, and during the course of our communications, he was also elected President of the Health Care Compliance Association (HCCA). Odell has held government enforcement and top compliance positions and is a great example of someone who has had a successful career working in internal compliance positions. Currently, Odell serves as President of the Society of Corporate Compliance and Ethics (SCCE) and Past President of HCCA.

Rodney Smith

Rodney Smith started out from college in the compliance field and works as a compliance analyst inside a company. Rodney has not been working in the field as long as some of our other contacts, and for that reason, many readers will find his insights especially engaging. Rodney joined the field through the environmental, safety and health side of the field and went looking for an ethical company with which to pursue his interest while he was still completing his education. He remained with the company after he finished his degree.

Joseph Murphy

Joe Murphy, popularly known as the Dean of Compliance, currently is of counsel to the firm of Compliance Systems Legal Group (CSLG), and is a Senior Advisor and co-founder of Integrity Interactive. Joe did compliance work in-house for twenty years and has written extensively in the field. Joe serves on the Board of Directors of HCCA and the Advisory Board of SCCE, and has earned that organization's professional credential, Certified Compliance and Ethics Professional (CCEP). Joe Murphy is one of this book's authors (though he did not write this description).

Linda Lipps

Linda Lipps earned her first compliance and ethics role—as have so many others in this field—by doing research and creating the program from the ground up. Since that time, Linda has gone on to hold other roles, and even helped start a compliance and ethics organization, known as the Greater Houston Business Ethics Roundtable (GHBER), for smaller businesses in Houston.

Richard Gruner

Richard Gruner is a law professor who also contributed to the Organizational Sentencing Guidelines, taking part in the Ad Hoc Advisory Group that developed the Guidelines' 2004 revisions. Richard makes a point of including compliance in his white-collar crime courses, and also seeks to contribute to the development of the field through writing and speaking engagements.

Special Thanks

We would like to take this opportunity to specially thank all the individuals who took time out of their busy schedules to help us with this project. Nearly everyone we contacted was willing and eager to participate, just as they were all quite open. Long after the interview process was completed, they continued to email us with resources and information relevant to the project. This book would not have been the same without their participation, and we hope their accounts can serve as great models for our readers.

Odell Guyton

Director of Compliance

1. **What is your current role in the compliance/ethics field: i.e., your title, employer, and city where you work?**

I'm the Director of Compliance for Microsoft Corporation. It's a global role, in terms of making sure that Microsoft as a company maintains and implements a world-class, effective compliance program, based on the *U.S. Federal Sentencing Guidelines*. This program is to be one that meets or exceeds existing government guidance and best practice on a worldwide basis. We're located in Redmond, Washington, United States of America.

2. **What do you *do* in your job? How do you spend most of your time? What people do you interact with?**

The time I spend is really involved with a lot of senior executives at the company both in promoting and educating, making them and other employees aware of what compliance means and what we do as a group. We are also being partners with them. When I say partners, I mean that in a broader sense, in terms of assisting them in navigating through some of the complexities of this compliance area. We're exposing them to how compliance touches their day-to-day work, and how we can be useful in making their work less risk-full, from a compliance-risk perspective, as well as providing guidance with regard to policies and company positions that they may not be exposed to on a regular basis, or have specific knowledge about.

We are keen on developing training programs that are designed to increase the awareness of our colleagues around the world about compliance issues (and also legal risk issues), and to act as a resource for them to obtain substantial guidance in how to avoid problems. That's what most of my time is spent on, interacting with these individuals, interacting with my staff and making sure that they're on top of things that come through—project management. Then we have outside interests in terms of making sure that government knows that we are a company that cares about compliance and that we not only talk about being in compliance, but we actually live it, and that we are able to effectively and objectively demonstrate these precepts. So that's most of my day. Other parts are spent in responding to reports or allegations relevant to compliance concerns, and then the ventures within the company as well as those outside the company.

3. Do you personally do much in the way of public speaking and presentations?

Yes I do, and that's a requirement of my role, as well. I speak in public, in the broader sense, in terms of being an advocate or ambassador for Microsoft's program; and also internally, around the world speaking to internal audiences about the existence of the program, about who I am, what my role is, and what the role of the compliance function is. I'm also speaking to executives worldwide, to make sure that they understand the importance that the Board and that Bill Gates and Steve Ballmer place on this program. And also getting them to contribute into that exercise where we talk about it as *tone at the top*, understanding that they have a direct responsibility and accountability for making sure their actions are in compliance and that the company that they represent is in compliance.

4. How did you get into the field? What attracted you? And how long have you been in this field?

The field is a pretty broad one, so if we define the field in my case: I'm a practicing attorney, and as attorneys, we all have a fiduciary obligation for compliance. Comply with the law, seek justice, be ethical, push yourself to a higher standard, and be knowledgeable about the subject matter: those are all precepts of the law. In a broader sense, as an attorney serving two independent careers as a prosecutor in some very highly regarded offices of the government (the Philadelphia District Attorney's Office as well as the United States' Attorney's Office in Philadelphia, Department of Justice), I guess I've been in compliance for a long time. When I left the U.S. Attorney's Office, I went into private practice for a number of years and represented corporate executives and corporations and defended clients that were accused of wrongdoing, and also began a practice where we focused on what I would describe as "preventative law." Making clients aware that simple actions, if taken the wrong way, with the wrong motivation, could lead to serious problems and having processes in place to first recognize the pitfalls, and then to avoid them and to factor in compliance concerns into the business operations.

While at the private practice, I was offered a unique opportunity to continue the implementation of the University of Pennsylvania's compliance program. Being the corporate compliance officer for the university and for the health system certainly exposed me to the intricacies in the roles of internal audit and compliance. So, I got out of the legal field, per se, into the finance and internal audit field, and then had the other fortunate opportunity of being asked by Microsoft to continue that work for this global company on a different scale. In all, I guess I've been in the field of compliance since about the beginnings of my law school career, which was in 1979, until present.

I have also just recently been elected to the position of President of the Health Care Compliance Association. So there I am also associated with other individuals in the field who have achieved positions of trust among the membership and amongst other fields of compliance. Having the ability and the honor to provide leadership and guidance to my colleagues outside of Microsoft is very humbling. I learn from every one of those people, every one of my colleagues. I think as compliance professionals, we also have a role to mentor others in the field, and to promote the profession. Not just by speech, but by substantive word, and deed. To give others a leg up, and to use our influence to make others achieve the next level. Give them the benefit of our knowledge, so to speak.

5. **As far as HCCA is concerned, do you have prior experience with health care companies, or is your experience more along the compliance side, so that you are not actually dealing in the business of health care?**

Well, yes, I have experience in the health care side. The University of Pennsylvania role was not only as corporate compliance officer for the university, but also as corporate compliance officer for the University of Pennsylvania health system. In private practice, I certainly was involved very substantially in Federal False Claims Act cases, which during that time were primarily focused in health care organizations. So yes, I have experience in compliance both on the health care side, as well as from the other side.

6. **What are your thoughts on how your background in law and government affected your move into other compliance positions?**

The law, whether it's a statute or regulation or guidance, always sets the minimum standard or expectation that society is willing to accept for conduct. So, having been at that perspective, where you prosecuted people or defended people that either have crossed a line or have come so close to the line that it becomes a question of fact whether they crossed the line, you tend to understand people's motivations. You understand that if we're dealing with corporations, the fact that people act as agents of their companies means that they cause companies to be in violation of the law. And defending those who weren't the actual actors but are now receiving the negative publicity or potential criminal or civil liability because of the actions of an employee or an executive, you see the human side as well. You see the side where people who really want to do good are now being punished for the acts of either reckless people or people that intended to violate the law for their own self-motivation. So, in terms of making sure that innocent people aren't harmed by these situations, the best way to think about it is in terms of prevention. And the experience that I've had as both a prosecutor and defense attorney gave me such a unique perspective, an invaluable perspective. It would be important that you have some resource that also can give you that practical legal experience.

In terms of other professions, I'm not suggesting that you can't be a good, or exceptional compliance officer or professional without being a lawyer. I'm not saying that at all. I'm just saying the law does provide you a worldview of many of the issues and the problems that are going to become public or have severe impact to your employer or to you personally. So it's good to be able to be in a position to predict or forecast that if you traveled on this particular road it's likely to lead you to a bad place, whereas if you take another particular road, it's likely to lead you to a better place. So I think that my experience in terms of being part of the legal profession is invaluable. Plus, there's the fact that the legal profession has always had tenets of ethics, both from an aspirational standpoint and a discipline standpoint, such that you have a system where if you do things wrong as an attorney, you can be disciplined, you can be excluded from the profession. That's highly valuable; the only other comparable one is the medical profession. I'm not sure that the CPA accounting world has gotten to that level of discipline, but I think that becomes important in the space of compliance.

7. How would you describe financial treatment in the field?

Well, I don't know. It's hard to calculate it in terms of that, because it depends on what value your employer places on compliance, your level in the organization, your skill set, and what your potential for advancement is. So it's hard to put a monetary value on it, but clearly you can make a good living as a compliance officer; a few are in those higher-salary ranges. It certainly provides you an opportunity to move from a lower salary to a more lucrative salary simply because of the demand in the industry and the present climate that we're in.

So I can only answer that question that it's a good field that's now probably hitting pretty high demand for people with particular talents, who have positioned themselves with their abilities to be attractive to companies that need that specific talent. And in a variety of industries, not just health care, of course, but banking, manufacturing, technology, software development, auditing, etc. It certainly is crossing many fields. And these are transferable skills, so you don't have to pigeonhole yourself. Just because you have experience in health care doesn't mean you can't effectively use those same experiences that you earned as a compliance professional in health care into the banking world or into the manufacturing world.

8. **There is a lot of demand right now. The scandals have given the field a lot of public attention and made boards want to be very public about supporting it, so how is job security? Do you see that changing in the future?**

Job security is an interesting way to phrase it. I don't know that any one of us has real job security. A good mentor of mine in the legal profession that I always respected once told me that, "Every lawyer must be prepared to pack his bags and leave." I guess that's true for compliance professionals as well. Every compliance professional must be prepared to pack their bags and leave if there's a situation that comes up in the course of your role that you, from an ethical, legal, integrity standpoint, can't tolerate (or if management isn't handling it in a manner that you feel is responsible). I also don't think many companies are going to go about firing their compliance officers or their compliance directors, because that would certainly create a hum in their various industries.

9. **Not necessarily looking at your current position, but perhaps at people who are compliance officers in general, or people who are looking to move to other positions, do you think that there is a lot of mobility required?**

I think mobility is relevant; you may have a lot of opportunity but your personal circumstances may limit your mobility. You might have family matters that keep you in one area, so you're not able to accept an opportunity. I would say the compliance profession is one that has a pretty robust set of opportunities that may be available for those with the appropriate skill set. And in this climate, those opportunities are really more abundant, more visible, more desirable in terms of corporate thinking now than they were, let's say, 5 or 10 years ago. The mobility question is really one of personal situation. But I would advise, in order to get those top jobs, those quality positions, you would restrict your ability to get those if you were less mobile than the next candidate. These are worldwide opportunities, and that's why mobility does become a factor.

10. **Looking at the types of skills that come into play in the field and the type of work that you do, is there a field that you would compare it closely to?**

I talked about the law. That certainly is a comparable field. Internal audit, or audit, certainly is a comparable field. If you're talking about the desire to do good as a motivator, certainly the medical field becomes a parallel, the legal field is a parallel, and prosecutors are a parallel. There are a number of these associated fields that would call on the same type of ethical qualities.

11. **And those kinds of people would be most likely to be drawn to compliance work?**

People that want to make a meaningful change for the greater good, whatever that greater good is, I think those are the people that are probably drawn to compliance work.

12. What are the gratifying parts of working in the field?

I would say, to see meaningful change in a culture of a group. A "culture" meaning attitude, empowerment, making it better, having an impact, an influence, in moving them from point zero to positive point 15 or 20 or 100 in a short period of time. That's gratifying. Saving someone's job if they get into an issue where management has misread the concern. Making sure people do have a voice, in terms of not necessarily being an advocate or ombudsman. But that where they see issues that cause them concern, that they have an opportunity to raise it without them being subject to the whims of management just because they raised the initially possible compliance concern. And having the ability to provide them some avenue of protection against retaliation/retribution, that type of thing. It's all gratifying; at the end of the day, when you come home you may be tired, you may have other issues to deal with, but at least you know that, for the most part, you do have the opportunity to make a positive impact.

13. What are the things that you look back on that were frustrating?

It can vary. It can vary. You can have a good day and have it be very frustrating, and you can have a bad day and have it be even more frustrating. Or you can have a day where nothing happened and it can be frustrating; that's the more difficult part of it. It depends on how you look at it.

14. In other words, it depends on how much you let things bother you?

Yes, how much you let things bother you, how quickly you want things to change. Sometimes you can keep hammering and hammering and change doesn't come, if at all, for a very long time. So during the time that you're hammering you may be frustrated, but when you see a little change, you might be feeling good about it. So it all seems relative. I don't think anybody's in a job to make them happy. My wife would always say to me, "Does your job make you happy?" I'd say, "That's really not an appropriate question." I don't enter into a job for it to make me happy. I enter into marriage to make me happy. I plan to have a family to make me happy, but I never viewed a job as making me happy. I guess if I had a job where it was a hobby, and now I'm making money from my hobby, that would certainly make me happy, but I don't know if you can find that in the compliance field. Or any field, actually.

15. What opportunities for advancement do you see? And you can think about the ones that are there for say, chief compliance officers (if there are higher opportunities), or where else there is potential growth within the field.

You don't have to be at the Chief Compliance Officer level or Director of

Compliance level to have those things be available to you. There is plenty of opportunity at the implementation levels in many organizations that either becomes the stepping stones for other things, or provides you with opportunities to learn about operations of a business or function of a business that you could be exposed to in the compliance realm. Particularly now that enterprise-wide risk management becomes an integral part of the process of compliance. I think that's an exciting way to understand and appreciate business: the rhythm of the business, the entity, who makes it up, what are the functions of other roles in the business, what are the cycles, those types of things.

There's probably a larger, more visible opportunity now in multi-national corporations, in publicly traded corporations, primarily because of the impact of Sarbanes-Oxley. But then you have other laws that are coming into play at the state and local levels that are emphasizing compliance and emphasizing corporate ethics, company ethics, company compliance. You have things that are occurring in companies now that show a greater sensitivity/visibility to ethical conduct: not necessarily conduct that violates a legal standard, but conduct that violates ethical-sensitivity precepts. Anyway, opportunities abound, and drawing on what I said earlier, this is a good time for compliance professionals. We just can't afford to lose it, or to not seize the day.

16. How do you feel about external positions, such as in consulting or service providers?

These peripheral, outside, or on-the-edge companies also create opportunity. It's like a feeding frenzy; no one's going to be left out. The broader it is, the better it is. Just in the years that I've been at Microsoft, I've seen so many more, what I would have called "peripheral" organizations now becoming primarily or more focused on compliance. The risk management components, for example, they never really thought of compliance. There are just more insurance groups that are now thinking about compliance. Lawyers, general counsels, are now thinking beyond legal risk and looking at compliance. The finance professionals, the controllers, CFOs, CEOs, boards of directors: they're now having meaningful discussion about compliance, and realizing the consequences from non-compliance. The internal auditors are now factoring in situations that create compliance risk in terms of the balance sheet. Management's now being weighed and assessed on their ethics and their ability to comply with codes of conduct. I think this is tremendous.

17. What would you recommend to those who are interested in getting into this field? Have you ever been in a position to hire for compliance positions?

Oh, certainly, yes.

18. What things do you look for? What would you suggest to someone who wanted to get into one of those positions?

The things I look for are: a keen interest, defined by motivation, spirit/energy, willingness to learn, a humbleness—I'm turned off by people who think they know it all; ability to communicate well at multiple levels; ability to understand; ability to appreciate different cultures. I look at people who are able to communicate well, both spoken communication and non-verbal communication. I look for substantive knowledge; I look for organization skills, project management skills—people that aren't going to get lost in the forest or give you that "deer in the headlights" look. These are the types of things that I look at.

19. Are there any resources that you wish had been available to you when you were first taking compliance positions?

Well, I wish I had had more exposure to the world of corporate finance: the law of corporations, the importance of shareholders, etc. But sometimes the best learning is on the job.

20. You are very high up in the HCCA; what about organizations like it. Can they be useful to job seekers?

The EOA [now ECOA], SCCE, and the other organizations are fine organizations of the highest caliber. The memberships of those organizations are some of the finest people I've come to know and am partners with. You cannot do wrong by joining a professional association, where you can connect with those in higher positions/in parallel positions, and have a fellowship, if you will, of professional connectivity. Because they're going through the same things you're going through. And just to have someone that understands these things at a different level, at a more intimate level, you may get an idea that you didn't think of. You may pick up a practice that you didn't think of; you may see a different slant on how to do a particular issue or problem solve that you hadn't thought of before. So communication is key, even amongst peers. You're going to share candidly best practices, and to discuss frustrations. This provides you some support and some knowledge, that others that you respect, and who have significant skills, are successful in dealing with the issues that you are having trouble with. There are all kinds of intangible rewards that come from being part of these memberships in a meaningful way: not just going to conferences and listening to someone ramble on, but functional interaction. That recognition, from others that are in the same field, that says, "Hey, this is important," that underscores or reassesses for you that the work you do is important.

21. Is there any educational background that you would recommend? For instance, do you think that it is best to get a law or business degree?

A law degree has worked for me; it may not work for the next person. If you have an aptitude for business school, that'd be great. I don't know; one size doesn't fit all. It's more of a combination of your substantive learning and your personality that really, in my view, makes the day. Rather than what you decided to do when you were 17 or 18 in terms of getting the college degree or getting the graduate degree.

22. If five years from now, someone were to walk in and they had a degree in compliance and business ethics, would they get any consideration above someone who say, just had a degree in law or a degree in business administration, for instance?

Oh, I have no idea. I've never hired anyone just based on their degree; I hire people on the whole person. I've taken chances on people that haven't had any formal training in compliance, because I knew that they had the ability and aptitude to understand (they would get the job done) over someone that had formal education in it. What can I say? I don't think that having any particular piece of paper is going to make you more marketable; it depends on the individual job.

23. So would you then put more value on work experience and if so, what would you recommend? Should you get into the industry before trying to get into compliance?

I would say you have to look at the whole person: their life experience, in combination with their work experience. You look at their work experience to determine if they have demonstrated aptitude and abilities in the job. You take a higher risk if they certainly don't have any experience in the job, but like anything, how much risk are you willing to take with a candidate? That's really what you're trying to assess and of course, you never really know about a person until they're in the job. You could have a person that has great abilities, looks good on paper, but can't get along with their fellow employees because they're terrible people-people. So it's really sometimes a crapshoot. But I think you have to look at the whole combination of the person, plus their references—what they've done throughout their lives (those are professional references and personal references). I think it's a holistic type of view you have to bring to the table.

24. What are the mistakes to avoid when you are getting into compliance?

You have to have perseverance, patience and the ability to think strategically and communicate. If you think things are going to happen overnight and people are going to reward you for your conduct, will recognize your contribution, then you probably shouldn't be in the field.

25. Are there any books or other readings that you would recommend on compliance?

I subscribe to *ethikos*; it's a very contemporary piece. It's a short read/a quick read from very professional people, and I certainly use that. The periodic BNA guides and things of that type, where you actually see real cases play out, and then following up on those squibs that come out in those, are effective. Then look at some of the Welch books from the former GE CEO—they have some value. Now there are books coming out on Corporate Social Responsibility, transparency, etc., that are probably worth the read just so you understand what people are predicting will be the future of the corporate world. Also, look at some of the emerging economies (China, India); that gives you a little bit of a glimpse into where things might be going.

Interviewed April 6, 2005

Rodney Smith
In-House Environmental, Health, Safety and Ethics Analyst

1. What is your current role in the compliance/ethics field: i.e. your title, employer, and city where you work?

My title is "Compliance Analyst." I work for the Timken Company, and it's in Canton, Ohio. Actually, technically North Canton, because I'm at the R&D center.

2. What do *do* in your work? How do you spend most of your time? What sorts of people do you interact with?

I would say a nice chunk of my time is done for training. I do business law and ethics training, though not comprehensively; I just get into a few of the topics, including Harassment Prevention, Foreign Corrupt Practices, Copyright Compliance, and Environmental Law. The majority of my educational emphasis is Environmental, Safety and Health, so occupational health, safety and environmental is what I specialize in. In addition to training, I do a lot of procedure writing, auditing. Those are my three primary roles: auditor, policy and trainer (to make sure they uphold the policies).

3. Do you just do that on-site, or do you do any traveling?

It is mostly on-site; I do some traveling. I should say that another one of my primary roles, and it kind of comes under the audit portion, is risk assessment. Since we're an R&D center, I'll look at new processes and products that we're developing from a risk standpoint: occupational safety health risk; environmental risk; not necessarily legal risk, per se, but mostly the environmental, safety and health. So if we're working with a machine tool builder, and they happen to reside in New York or somewhere else, I do travel to that facility to audit that before it ends up going to our manufacturing plant. I would say my travel's restricted to roughly 4-5 weeks a year, so I'm mostly here.

4. **How did you get into this field? What were your reasons? How long have you been working in it?**

If we go way back, coming out of high school I was very interested in wildlife and nature in general. I wanted to get into the environmental field, and there was a degree at my local community college called "Environmental Technology," so I'm thinking to myself, *oh, this must be what I want to do: this is Environmental.* So I went into that program and it turned out that it was environmental from the standpoint of the compliance side, and it wasn't environmental science. Then I was introduced to occupational health and safety, and I wasn't disappointed when I found out that it was a little different than I had anticipated; I actually liked it, so I stuck with it. I went into the Associate program, and I needed an internship in order to finish that, so that's how I got my foot in the door at Timken. I put in a resume; my primary objective on that resume was to find a positive-minded, ethical company to serve my internship with, and they hired me. So I finished out that degree. I've been with Timken five years; in that time, I finished my undergrad at the University of Akron, and with an emphasis in Emergency Management. That was a little bit different, so that expanded my background; I looked at natural hazards, even terrorism/homeland security, hazardous materials/fire. And I just finished up with my graduate degree in Environmental, Safety and Occupational Health from the University of Findlay. So I've been with Timken, as of the 22nd of this month, it will be exactly five years, if you include my internship. It's a good field to be in; I really enjoy the field.

5. **So having actively sought a job in this field, do you think that in doing preparation and taking these courses, you were better prepared than say, other people who have previously entered the field not really knowing what it was?**

    Oh absolutely. Definitely.

6. **How would you describe your financial treatment in this field? Do you see the pay in the field as more, less or comparable to others, based on the level you are in and those you are aware of?**

I would say it's extremely well compensated and rewarding, from a financial standpoint. I've looked at some statistics for other, prestigious-type jobs, and I think it pays very well; I've been rewarded well, going up the ranks. If you work hard, it doesn't matter what field you're in; they'll take notice of that. I think one of the biggest challenges from a financial standpoint is, showing them that you're not (and you really are in this position) "overhead." Showing them that you contribute to the bottom line is very important. That's key so that they know how much you're contributing to the company. That then, in turn, is rewarded, through your salary, when they see that you're saving the company money.

7. **You have come in recently, comparatively, and have seen some of the changes that the field has gone through since all these scandals have taken place, so you have had a fresher look at it. Do you think that the changing regulations and laws have had any effect on financial compensation, or is that something that is probably going to stay pretty steady, regardless of all that?**

I think the current climate does definitely have an effect on that; with scandals, the awareness is raised. Laws like Sarbanes-Oxley come forth, and things like that definitely do, I believe, affect it. It increases the awareness; any time there's a perception of higher risk involved, they want to avert that risk, mitigate it, so naturally you're going to be in a better position, financially.

8. **On a similar topic, how do you think job security is in the field? Is it different from other fields, because of the nature of it, or is it still dependent on performance, largely?**

I think the job security is good. They're always going to need folks in this position, as far as risk management is concerned; it's definitely going to be needed. Especially looking at it from the Environmental, Safety and Health standpoint, there's always going to be OSHA, there's always going to be EPA; on the ethical side, you're always going to have EEOC and all the different administrations that affect that. I think it's always going to be taken seriously and valued. So I don't see an issue there.

9. **On mobility, you already mentioned that you do some small amount of traveling, a few weeks a year, but do you think to advance within this field you have to be willing to travel? Or do you think you would be able to do that where you are?**

Yes, I think advancement definitely is going to correlate with travel. If I were to advance from here, I believe it would be a corporate position, so I'm going to be all over the globe. If I weren't willing to travel, that'd definitely be a hindrance to moving up. There's a direct relation there.

10. **Do you feel that, starting as you have at the position you are in, that you would be able to climb the compliance ladder and eventually become a high-ranking compliance officer with this company? Or do you think that you would have to go to a different company?**

No, I think I could do it where I am, definitely.

11. **What field would you compare this field most closely to? In other words, what other professionals & students would be likely to be drawn to compliance and ethics because of similar interests?**

I would say law would be pretty close. Naturally the curriculum's a little bit different; it's more law intensive than the curriculum I was used to with Risk Management in general. I know there are degree programs now just for risk management. So it doesn't necessarily matter exactly what context we're looking at—whether it be environmental risk, occupational health and safety, legal, ethical—but risk management in general is kind of its own genre now. So that would definitely be a close program. I don't know of any other ones directly that I would say are really closely related. Environmental, Safety and Health really is kind of its own program aside from some of the other ones that are out there, and that's the track I took. You get exposed to a little of the legal side, and the ethical side, so that's how I moved into that realm.

12. What is the most gratifying part of working in this field?

It's really gratifying because it's an altruistic cause. Definitely on the safety, occupational health and environmental side you can actually see the results. Unlike some jobs, where it's kind of hidden and you don't necessarily see exactly what the results are, in this case you know what you're doing is a good cause; it's helping people. You can see the results. I find that very rewarding.

13. What is the most frustrating part?

That is definitely human nature, psychology/organizational psychology. You can be good at policy writing and administering your program to uphold those policies, but naturally there's always the human element. And people do what they want; you always get the non-compliant ones. It's a constant battle. You have to have a good discipline policy, up front; just getting other people who don't want to necessarily go along is one of the more frustrating parts of it.

14. What do you see as the opportunities for advancement working as a compliance analyst, and also within the industry? Where do you see the most potential growth in compliance as a whole?

Definitely on the ethical side there's a great awareness. So we might see a lot of growth there. Also on the Environmental, Safety and Health side, there's definitely growth. Homeland Security, especially after 9/11 when the federal government formed the Homeland Security Department. There are colleges all over the country now that are coming up with programs like this, so it's growing very rapidly. The awareness of it is going down to the elementary school level now. They're trying to get young folks aware of it, so it's growing very fast. Whereas, when I did my undergrad in Emergency Management, it was at one of two schools in the country that even had a program. Now I believe there're about twenty. It's growing very fast because of the awareness of situations like that, and the risk.

15. As far as opportunities, do you see much value to outside companies, consulting firms, product companies, within compliance?

Yes, definitely, especially within consulting firms. There's a great need for that. A lot of companies now turn to consulting firms for compliance needs; there's not always an in-house compliance officer, so sometimes companies, I've seen, rely solely on outside folks. Consulting is definitely a big opportunity, but also within the corporation; there's still a lot of opportunity there, as positions are created.

16. What do you recommend to people who are interested in getting into the field? You can speak to attitudes, skills, etc. What should people be doing if they are interested in the field? What should they be looking for in themselves?

I think it definitely takes a very self-directed person (someone who's very forward, definitely a positive attitude), because there are going to be challenges. And folks have to be willing to deal with challenges, take that energy and use it in a constructive way. Attitude is everything. It really takes a positive-minded, strong person, someone who doesn't need a lot of directives. If someone likes to be managed and told what to do, there's a good chance they wouldn't want to go into this field. It takes someone who pretty much can take care of themselves: they know what needs to be done. They can analyze the program and figure out where the gaps are and take it on, without being told. Especially in this position, because if a company hires a compliance officer, they don't want to be involved with the details. They don't want to micro-manage the program; they want someone that's self-directed, that'll just take it on, tackle the problems, administer the program for them so that they don't have to worry about it. Yeah, definitely a self-directed, ambitious, positive-minded type person.

17. What educational background do you recommend for those who are interested in getting into this field? You can speak to both your industry/ environmental-related and then also in general.

On the environmental, safety and health side, it's good to have a really firm legal background. At least a pretty good understanding of engineering, as well, because they have to be able to look at things in industry, and construction even, and understand how it works. Financial analysis is important: being able to speak in dollars and show what needs to be done, and what the results are. Project management's very important: being able to tackle projects, understand how they're done, and achieve results. It depends really on the track they want to go on. If they want to go the environmental track like I did, they definitely want to go for that type of degree, but there needs to be a lot of business integrated into that. Organizational psychology, understanding cultures—just really a myriad of things. And that's one of the things I love about this; really, you need to have a very, very broad background in order to do it well. Understand psychology, sociology, the financial side of things (accounting, legal) etc.

18. **A lot of people believe a Liberal Arts education is one of the best ones to prepare you for compliance. Obviously speaking and writing are going to be chief parts of any role in compliance, and then you need to be able to sell, because even if you are not selling a product, you are still selling the program and selling the concepts within the program.**

Exactly, that's very important. Even understanding personality types can be extremely helpful. The Myers-Briggs indicator, if you understand how that works and how people work, you're able to sell to them. If you can pin someone down within a few minutes and understand who they are, you can definitely tailor what you're saying, so it sells. You've got to be a salesman in this field, too. Writing, definitely. You need strong grammar and writing skills.

19. **On work experience, is there a specific path that is good to take? Should someone try to get into the industry that they are interested in or try to go straight into a compliance program?**

I would say go straight in. I haven't really seen the other side; I've gone straight into compliance. I'm trying to think about it from another standpoint. It's not to say that someone with a different background couldn't go into compliance; I know a lot of people in the field have very diverse backgrounds. I've seen some successful people in compliance that started out as teachers, as a matter of fact, which is interesting. I've seen a lot of occupations, and they decided they needed something different. They scooted into this field, and they're doing well at it. It really depends on the individual.

20. **Do you think it is more difficult to get hired into compliance or ethics fresh out of college than other fields, because of the relative freshness of the field, the relative lack of courses and experience, etc.?**

I wouldn't say that it's that huge of a challenge, actually, because I think it's well recognized, at least in industry, that compliance is important. It seems well known; it's not really emerging to the point that it's not understood. I think it is. So I don't think that's really that big of a challenge. There's enough curriculum out there, enough schools now that have it, that the educational opportunity's out there, and I think the employment follows.

21. **What kind of mistakes should someone try to avoid when they are getting into the field? What mindsets or choices can hinder success?**

They definitely have to be open-minded. A huge mistake would be to be close-minded, not willing to change, because you are going to be challenged, constantly. If you come up with a solution or program you think will work, there are always going to be people that tell you it won't. They'll have good reasons why, and you need to be able to defend yourself without being close-minded. You have to be really open-minded to all possible alternatives. There are a lot of ways to approach any single problem, and a lot of solutions. You have to be extremely creative with some of the solutions when it comes to compliance. Especially when the law's not entirely defined. It's not always concise; it doesn't tell you what to do. It just leaves it open-ended, sometimes. So in situations like that, the person has to be willing to work with other people, be a team player and be open-minded. Always open.

22. Are there any books or other readings that you would recommend, or have had recommended to you, about the field?

Some publications/organizations on the environmental, safety and occupational health side include Occupational Hazards (www.occupationalhazards. com), Compliance Magazine (www.compliancemag.com/), Environmental Protection Magazine (www.eponline.com/), and the American Society of Safety Engineers (Professional Safety Journal), Board of Certified Safety Professionals, American Industrial Hygiene Association ("Synergist" magazine for Industrial Hygienists), et al. But on the ethical side, and legal side, I don't know as much as I'd like to. I'm sure there are some publications out there, and I haven't really gotten into it (and even certifications).

23. Looking back at when you were getting into the field, when you were making your choices, are there any resources that you wish you had had, and are any of those available yet?

A book like what you're coming out with would have been nice. Something that gave me an overview of what's going on in the field, what kind of actions I should take, things to focus on, from an educational standpoint and as far as a personal standpoint, resources. Pretty much what you're doing is what I would've liked to have had. But like I said, I got pieces and parts. I asked people a lot of questions and kind of pieced everything together. Right now I think it's still kind of that way. There's kind of a conglomerate of resources, but nothing that's pulling it all together and saying, "Here we go, here's a pretty good guide you can use." It'd be nice to have that.

24. When you were trying to find a company that you wanted to work with and do your internship with, were you able to talk to people in compliance programs already? Were there people who were able to give you advice?

No. It would have been nice, though, for sure.

25. All right, do you have any final comments on working in the field/starting a career in the field?

No, other than again, just ambition, positive-mind, being open; there's a lot that goes into it. People have to be willing to take it on and stay with it, really. It's not as focused as a lot of occupations. There are many occupations where you can really focus on what it is, and it's cut and dry, but this one's definitely not. It's always evolving. I check the Federal Registrar on a daily basis, and you have to. You have to stay up to date, always be watchful, and keep an eye on what's going on. That's a big part of it.

Interviewed May 16, 2005

Joseph "Joe" Murphy

Former In-House Compliance Lawyer; Outside Lawyer, Compliance Advisor

1. What is your current role in the compliance/ethics field: title, employer, and city where you work?

I am of counsel to a compliance law firm, Compliance Systems Legal Group (CSLG). I am also a Senior Advisor and co-founder of Integrity Interactive Corporation, the leader in online compliance training. I am also co-editor of *ethikos*, a bi-monthly publication devoted to practical approaches to business ethics and compliance. My office is in Haddonfield, New Jersey, a small town near Philadelphia, Pennsylvania.

2. What do you *do* in your job? How do you spend most of your time?

In my role in CSLG I provide advice to companies. Much of this I can do from my office, on the phone or by email. I may write or review draft company documents—codes, policy statements, audit reports—and provide the client with changes and ideas. I also do training and audits for companies. The training involves on-site visits and presentations to employees. These sessions are typically interactive, using exercises like role-plays or other techniques to involve the employees in the learning process. The audits also involve on-site visits including review of documents and interviews with employees, as well as walking the premises. I also participate in client meetings addressing a variety of compliance program elements.

As part of my work I also spend time promoting the compliance field and publicizing the firm. All of us at CSLG do public speaking at compliance symposia, and write articles and books on a variety of aspects of compliance and ethics.

In my role at Integrity Interactive, I work on a variety of matters, especially course development and review. I keep Integrity informed of important developments in the compliance field. I have also been involved with Integrity's compliance officer in developing their corporate compliance program. While I am in constant contact with Integrity, this is primarily done from my office.

3. How would you describe your role in this field?

One of my roles in this field is to ask difficult questions, and to challenge people to take a tougher and more realistic approach. When I started in the field, most of what was done could basically be considered paper and preaching. You'd have lawyers writing documents and lawyers going out and giving talks about what the law was and, unfortunately, a similar pattern in the ethics field. You'd have people essentially preaching, or playing values games, or stump-the-ethicists games. My ongoing role in this field is in part, to ask difficult questions about, "What are you doing to audit compliance? Will your audits actually find problems? Are you disciplining people for failure to take steps to prevent violations? Are you actually monitoring this conduct? Are you publicizing discipline? Does your incentive system really have an impact?" So part of it is asking those questions and part of it is providing very nitty-gritty, real-world advice on *how to get the job done*.

As I've said many times in speaking, my favorite audience is always the people who do the day-to-day work. That's really my strongest interest; it's the practical side. I've given a lot of thought to the theoretical side, a lot of thought to where compliance and ethics is coming from, how it fits in with society, but my favorite part of this field is the day-to-day, how-to piece. So a major part of what I do is looking for practical ways to get things done. Sometimes I do this through *ethikos*: if I hear somebody say something that I think is a really good idea, well then we'll turn it into an article for *ethikos*. Sometimes I do it in individual consulting and work for companies; sometimes I'll do it in developing a template for people so they have an easier way of getting the job done. I think my biggest contributions are asking difficult questions, to get people to think a little bit more, and trying to give them real practical, nuts-and-bolts advice on how to get the job done.

4. How did you get into the field? Why?

After a couple years in a law firm I took a job as an inside lawyer at one of the Bell companies working on antitrust. I was immediately involved in antitrust compliance work, including training and systems to ensure that competitors who needed our facilities were treated fairly. I discovered that there were people in the company whose mission was to see to it that the company did the right thing. And this was when Bell was first dealing with competition, and I was surprised to find that there were people in the company whose job it was to protect competition, to make sure the company did not misuse its dominant position in the marketplace. Not only did these people do this job, they believed in it. They took it very seriously, and I found that very interesting, and in a real sense, very inspiring. It became a model for me, a mental picture I always had of these people doing this difficult work, *and* they were not the officers of the company. They were not the presidents and the vice-presidents; they were mid-level managers who had this charge, who had this responsibility, and were quite serious about it. I liked the idea of fighting the good fight to ensure that the company did the right thing. I was hooked. That was the initial driver for me.

I also liked the idea of doing the right thing, even in the business environment. This field presented a way to work in the business world, and still have that commitment to doing the right thing. It was an area where I felt I could make a contribution.

5. How would you describe your financial treatment in this field?

One of the great things about this field is that you can devote yourself to getting people to do the right thing, yet be paid well. Whether it was working in-house, or being a lawyer at CSLG, I have been pleased with the financial treatment (pay and benefits). In my travels I have the sense that people in-house in this field are treated well.

Probably the best paid positions are those at companies that have been through a compliance disaster. After a company has been prosecuted and attacked in the press they are usually ready to spend real money on compliance, and to bring in people who will help improve their image.

It is also possible to do well outside of a company, in providing services like consulting and training. Of course, in starting up a business there is always an element of uncertainty initially but as long as you are comfortable with that it can be well worthwhile. Plus, you have a degree of independence doing that.

6. How is the job security in this field? Is mobility required?

I have worked in compliance for 30 years and have never had to move. As for security, in today's environment working for a large company is not as certain as it may have been in prior generations. Of course, any time there is a merger or acquisition you can expect consolidation, even in the compliance and ethics office. Compliance also has the risk that it is not a revenue generator but a cost center. On the other hand, when the specter of the government is at the door, companies retain compliance people. My assessment is that there is at least as much security in this field as there is in other important company functions. And, after Enron, that security has improved.

On the issue of mobility, this really depends on who the employer is and where you are working. If you are the compliance officer in a business unit far from headquarters and you want to become the corporate compliance officer, a move will be necessary. This is probably the norm for many types of management positions in larger companies with multiple locations. But it is not the general experience in compliance that practitioners are required to move an unusual amount.

7. What field would you compare this field most closely to?

My answer to this may come as a surprise. I see the most important task of compliance to be the prevention and early detection of the misuse of power in organizations. So to me the closest similar field is political science: the study of the use, misuse, and control of power.

On a more mundane level, compliance has some strong similarities to internal audit, and has some elements in common with risk management. It also has close ties to the overall field of management. Law is an obvious area as well, since much of this field deals with what the law requires. But the comparison can be overstated. It does not help much in this area merely to know the law, if you do not know how to translate that knowledge into action. Lawyers give legal advice; compliance and ethics people have to translate that into things that really affect what companies do.

On an academic level, organizational dynamics is very close to compliance. It is also important to remember that there are specialty areas in this field. If your focus is on environment, health and safety, then something in the health or environmental sciences may be closer to your field. If your area is health care compliance, then the field of medicine may be closely related to your work.

8. How has your perception of the field changed over the years?

I initially started doing this in the antitrust field, particularly focused on the laws dealing with monopolization. As I did a little bit of work in other fields (environmental, Foreign Corrupt Practices, Conflicts of Interest, Regulatory), I gradually started to see it (compliance itself) as a field. Also over time, I've become even more and more convinced of the need to focus on this from a political point-of-view, to look at controls on power. I've seen abuses that, even I, as kind of a paid skeptic, didn't expect. I didn't expect to see on such a wholesale level, senior executives involved in violations. I always expected some; I did not expect it on as massive a scale as I've seen it in the Enron era. So it's only tended to reinforce my view that you really have to work at controls. But the answer to the compliance and ethics field has never been, and never will be, paper and preaching; it will never be resolved by writing codes and training people. You absolutely need to do that—it's necessary—but never will it be sufficient to prevent misconduct and wrongdoing. You've got to use practical management tools; you've got to use controls that address the issue of the use and abuse of power.

I also see more and more a need to professionalize this field, and to strengthen it. People doing compliance work have a very difficult job. They are being called upon to meet the enormous challenge of preventing and detecting all forms of unethical and illegal conduct in organizations. They need all the support they can get, but they are not getting it. They are not getting the support they need from government; government is not doing anywhere near what it needs to do.

Government needs to do more to recognize compliance programs and compliance professionals. For example, if you look at the Sarbanes-Oxley Act, you will not find any reference to compliance programs or compliance officers, even though this law deals with preventing corporate misconduct. This omission is a mistake. Government needs to make it clear that it will treat companies better if their compliance programs are rigorous and staffed by empowered compliance professionals. Government also needs to take steps to eliminate the legal barriers to having effective compliance programs. It should be clear, for example, that the results of compliance audits cannot be used against companies.

Compliance and ethics people have not been getting the support they need from their profession; there's much more we need to professionalize this field. We need to provide good, solid ethics standards for people in this field, and there's a need to identify this field as a field. That is a critical issue. The compliance and ethics community and our membership organizations should be promoting our profession. They should work to promote strong ethical standards and they need to be an active voice with the government.

The people who are doing this work need to see themselves in a larger context as practicing in the field of ethics and compliance. They need their employers and society to recognize this as a discrete and very important field of practice, and that it is becoming truly a profession. It is necessary because the people doing this work need that degree of protection; they need that degree of independence and empowerment if they are going to work effectively. It is important to visualize the challenges confronted by compliance and ethics people. What I picture is the image of some very strong-willed, powerful senior-executive—you could easily picture this at some of the high-profile companies that have been in the news for compliance debacles. I picture the instance where this top-level person, who's always used to getting his or her way, is saying, "Don't give me your nonsense. This is how I want it done." And the compliance person being able to stand there, toe to toe, and say, "No, we're not doing it that way, and if you proceed, I have to go to the audit committee." And the compliance person will know that the audit committee will back him up, and the person will not be at risk of losing his job. Frankly, that's not the case, in most of Corporate America. Even in the best companies, you're not going to see very many compliance people who are in a strong enough position where they could do that. They might want to, but they're not given the resources and the authority that they need to take that position. I think over time it will change, because it has to change.

9. What is the most gratifying part of working in this field?

To me, the best part of this job is knowing that what I do can make a difference in people's lives. If a compliance program prevents one death from an industrial accident, or one worker's life being shattered by sexual harassment, or one manager being disgraced by involvement in a corporate fraud, then those of us who do this work have made an important contribution. We are helping people do the right thing, and helping those who believe in doing the right thing to win the tests of strength in their companies.

I also need to add that working with the people who are part of this field is one of the best parts of this profession. Compliance and ethics people share an important common bond. We have been through common experiences and easily share what we have learned with our peers. The people I have known have been very open in talking about what they are doing, and letting others learn from their successes and failures. We can find support and validation from our peers, when sometimes our employing companies need a little more convincing to understand what we are trying to do.

10. What is the most frustrating part of being in this field?

The greatest frustration comes from those who just don't get what this is about. They include the lawyers who see this cynically as merely an insurance policy, and the judges and plaintiffs' lawyers who see compliance programs as merely a source of litigation cannon fodder generated by us dumb corporate types who seem to conduct audits and write policies just so they can use them against us in litigation. There are the ethical purists who believe that all we need do is to teach business people the wisdom of business ethics, or who think "the answer" is just to be sure we hire ethical people and all will be well. There are the prosecutors who think that just a few more years of prison time and another few million in corporate fines will finally change the patterns of organizational corruption. In other words, it is surprisingly difficult for many people to understand what corporate compliance is about.

11. What do you see as the opportunities for advancement in your area? Where do you see the most potential growth?

There are some compliance areas that are always there, and where the need for experts is widespread: environment, workplace safety, product safety. But you also want to look at the trends: new enforcement areas, new areas of compliance focus. Right now, corporate governance is hot. Dealing with boards of directors, how you control executive misuse of power, how to satisfy the requirements of the Sarbanes-Oxley Act; these are all areas of growth.

Privacy is also an area that is likely to grow and become more complicated. It is a major compliance driver in Europe, and as technology tends to under-cut our personal privacy we can expect more government intervention. For example, companies are now facing new notification requirements if their data security is breached. It is also a universal risk area. Companies that deal with the public are especially at risk, but all companies have employees and they need to worry about protecting privacy in that context. Outside the U.S. some countries are even requiring companies to have privacy officers.

Another area that is now starting to develop is compliance programs in uni-versities. Initially such programs had been limited to the medical facilities, but the trend has finally caught on for the broader institutions. Universities are, in a real sense, often very large businesses with a broad range of compliance issues. They need to adapt to society's expectations in all these dealings with their con-stituencies. As we see more universities subject to embarrassing press reports of illegal or unethical conduct there will inevitably be increased impetus for the adoption of compliance and ethics programs.

It may not be possible to predict which risk areas and which types of busi-nesses will see the most future enforcement and compliance activity, but one thing that is sure: there will be new areas of focus in the future. There will be new series of scandals and increased enforcement. Often it only takes careful reading of sources like the *Wall Street Journal* to detect these trends.

12. Look forward 10, 20, 50 years—where do you see this field? What has changed? What still has not changed?

The need for the field will always be there, but I see it moving more in the direc-tion of becoming professional, a defined field. I see a day when people in college will say, "I really want to work in the compliance and ethics field, and I've got my career planned out, and here's what degree I'm going after. Here's how I'm going to do it." I see a point where, when Congress wants to do something affecting organizational conduct and they call witnesses, that the witnesses will include people in the ethics and compliance field (unlike the process that led to Sarbanes-Oxley). In fact, by that time, there may be people *in* Congress who started out in the ethics and compliance field. That would be a good development.

I see people in this field in all organizations, not just the for-profit companies, who are responsible for the job of managing effective compliance and ethics programs. I see them in universities, law firms, accounting firms, partnerships, non-profits, unions, and even government organizations. I see it absolutely on a global scale; I don't see anything in this entire field that's uniquely or distinctly American. I think it is a global trend.

What has not changed and will not change is the need for the fundamentals. Those in ethics and compliance will always need to be people of high integrity, with the strength of their convictions. They will always need to be able to get things done in organizations and to deal effectively with people. They will need a combination of optimism to believe that we can do better than we have, and enough skepticism to understand how much work it takes to achieve that goal.

13. What do you recommend to those who are interested in getting into this field?

I would advise talking with people who are already doing work in this field. There are many different types of positions. There are also significant differences in the companies' approaches to compliance. Don't judge the field by the first person you talk to or the first company you see. Also, read the books and articles on this field to learn what has gone on in the past. There is now quite a bit of written material available from those who have worked in compliance and ethics. I also recommend developing expertise in at least one of the risk areas. I did this initially in antitrust and FCPA, and then later in conflicts of interest and earnings management. Having that kind of additional depth can significantly enhance your value.

I always recommend doing writing in this field, since it is still a young, developing field. Someone interested in working in compliance and ethics could conduct a useful study on some of the important areas and make a contribution that would be useful to practitioners. Such writing credits would be an important addition to someone's resume. Doing research is also a good way to network with those already practicing in the field.

Another important strategy is to find a mentor or other form of partnership so you are working with others in this field in a collaborative way. The first book I wrote on compliance I did with my political science professor from Rutgers. I usually do major writing projects with others; we all learn from each other this way, and it makes the process more enjoyable.

14. What educational background do you recommend for those interested in getting into this field?

When we created the "compliance analyst" position in our firm, one of our preferred areas of background was political science. This reflects my own view that much of corporate compliance concerns the control of power—a political issue.

For someone starting new, my first recommendation would be a legal background. While compliance is not really the practice of law, some familiarity with law is a definite plus. But it is not essential.

Other useful background areas include audit and financial controls, and business and management, since so much of compliance relates to the ability to manage people and organizations. Of course, familiarity with other languages is a useful skill in multinational organizations.

Beyond this, there are a number of specialty compliance areas: environment, product safety, workplace safety, etc. In these areas background in the subject field is important. Thus, a compliance program dealing with safety in a nuclear facility would call for educational background in that field.

Some people believe business ethics is a good background. I am skeptical, because I think compliance and business ethics is more about understanding organizational dynamics, and less about mastering traditional ethics. But I would certainly give someone with an ethics background at least an interview in the hiring process.

15. What work experience would you recommend?

When a company gets into trouble they often want a shining knight to come to their rescue. If there were one type of experience I wish I had in my career, it would have been as a prosecutor. Being a former prosecutor, especially at the federal level, gives one enormous credibility. There is similar value in working at a regulatory agency, and then going into compliance work in that field. An enforcement background may also help you develop skill as an investigator, which is valuable background for compliance work.

In addition, there are a number of skills that are valuable in compliance: effective training of adults, personnel matters, auditing, investigating, clear writing, management leadership. Also, subject matter expertise and experience in compliance risk areas—environment, privacy, export control—help if your focus is those fields. Thus, if you wanted to do environmental compliance, having environmental engineering background would be very useful.

For certain positions, you can expect extensive work experience to be required. A major company is not going to hire someone as a compliance officer right out of college. Because compliance calls for management skills, it is useful to have experience in managing people and projects in a large organization. On the other hand, one of the newest developments in this field is the emergence of more and more junior level compliance positions. Increasingly it may become possible to pursue a career in the compliance field and work up to a compliance officer position.

16. What are the mistakes to avoid in getting into this field?

For many types of compliance positions it takes a certain personality. You have to be a true believer, someone who sees the value that compliance work can bring to both the employing organization and society in general. It is a mistake to go into this field thinking it is just a secure way to earn a living.

It is also important to know what you are getting into right from the beginning. Be skeptical. Also, make sure you get what you need right from the start. If you are offered a compliance position, make sure the company is really committed at the board and executive level. Also, try to get protection for your position in the company. Get this before you start; once you are in the job they will start to take you for granted, and it is much more difficult to get what you need.

17. What book or other reading would you recommend in this field?

There are several possibilities. As an editor of *ethikos* I recommend it strongly as a way to learn of new ideas and developments in this field. There is also the 1,000 page reference work Jeff Kaplan, Win Swenson and I did, although I am not sure there are many people who have the stamina to read it from beginning to end. On the lighter side, read some of the books on prior corporate scandals. So far, the best I have read recently is *The Smartest Guys in the Room*, by Elkind and McLean.

Interviewed December 29, 2004

Linda Lipps

Compliance Officer; Started In-House Compliance Program

1. How would you describe your current role in the compliance/ethics field? i.e., your title, employer and city where you work.

My title is Director of Ethics & Compliance for CenterPoint Energy in Houston. When I was with Waste Management, also in Houston, my title was Director, Corporate Ethics. My role as an Ethics Officer, with whatever company, gives me the opportunity to interact virtually with every aspect of that company. Because of the nature of my job, I am fortunate to be involved in numerous company meetings and initiatives outside the scope of my department.

2. **What would you say you *do* in your job? How do you spend most of your actual time?**

At Waste Management and here at CenterPoint Energy, I have a great deal of interaction with employees. By email, numerous phone calls, face to face meetings, reviewing cases that employees had called in through the helpline, following up on those cases, and working with other department heads incorporating ethics language and initiatives into their programs. The bulk of an ethics officer's day is going to be spent interacting with employees at one level or another. So at CenterPoint, the only thing that really has changed has been the title. There are similarities between all of our jobs as Ethics Officers, because most of our programs, if not all of the programs in corporate America, are pretty well structured under the Federal Sentencing Guidelines. There are going to be differences and a few tweaks and so forth but overall, it's very, very similar to what I was doing at Waste Management. The size of the company is different; CenterPoint Energy is a much smaller company. The industry of course is different. But again, the components that make up an ethics program are all very similar.

One of the first things I did when I got here was to outsource our Concerns Helpline; it had been implemented back in 2002, shortly after the Enron debacle and some of the others that catapulted so many companies into putting in helplines. It was being answered internally, but not by a live person: calls were going to a recorder. And while I know this is a standard practice for many companies, I'm concerned that some employees will not use a recorder. They can be fearful or apprehensive about tracing or tracking devices. And I think most people, for whatever reason you're calling someone, you really do like to get a live person.

So within the first month that I was here, we outsourced the helpline, which gives our employees 24/7 coverage, and language options for those callers that may be comfortable speaking in another language besides English. Also, by outsourcing to a vendor, we now provide a technology resource for employees that might be hearing disabled. So outsourcing is the best route to go for all of those reasons. We also put in a case management system, which is an essential component of any ethics office. I implemented TrakEnterprise, which is a software program that is used by the majority of ethics offices. It is a phenomenal system that helps you capture and track information from intake through multiple investigation steps through resolution and action taken. Those were the first two hot agenda items for me to get implemented once I was here. At the same time, we developed and documented new controls and processes.

Now I'm working on developing our ethics training for '06, which we roll out annually online. I'm also developing CenterPoint Energy's first conflict-of-interest questionnaire, which we will roll out in January of 2006. We are also working closely with H.R., Corporate Security, Internal Audit and others on many other projects such as policy reviews, job descriptions, incorporating ethics verbiage into our annual performance evaluation process, to name just a few. We will also be re-writing our Ethics Code of Conduct. So I am involved in working on all of the component pieces that make up an effective ethics office here at CenterPoint. But for me as an Ethics Officer – I'm just in a different industry, at a different company, with a different phone number. The job is still very much the same.

3. **Describe for me how you got into the field, why you made that choice and how long you have been working within the field?**

I've been in the Ethics arena since 1996. I was in an HR role with a large privately-owned company in Houston, and one of the principal owners came to me and said, "Linda, we're thinking about implementing a values-based ethics program, and I'd like for you to become involved and work with our general counsel on this." At the time, even from an HR perspective, to hear the term "values-based ethics program" was pretty unfamiliar. I really was clueless about what he was talking about, but I started doing some research, and of course, came across the Federal Sentencing Guidelines, and spent many hours talking with our general counsel. I decided this was something that was really intriguing to me, that I would enjoy doing, and could still use my people skills. Because I do think if somebody is looking at going into the ethics arena, that's almost a necessity (that you like people and that you want to be involved with people). This particular job would not be for someone that likes to sit in an office with their door closed all day and not have much interaction with anyone; it requires a lot of face time with individuals.

I started working with our general counsel, as well as our vice president of human resources, and spent a year just researching, because in 1996, there wasn't a whole lot out there. We joined the Ethics Officers Association; I remember the first EOA meeting I went to, we filled a large, private dining room in a hotel. Today, EOA has to search for a hotel property to host a conference in order to be able to accommodate everyone. Within the first year, I attended an executive course, co-hosted by Bentley College and EOA, near Boston called Managing Ethics in Organizations (MEO). So from research, the EOA, networking and an executive course, we started putting a program together: implementing a helpline, putting in a case management database, designing a code of conduct, and rolling out ethics training. I was with this company for five years. Then I received a call from Waste Management, a Fortune 200 company. So I went to Waste in July of 2000 and helped design and implement their program. I went from a small, privately owned, but very, very profitable company with less than 5,000 employees to a company that had, at that time, 55,000 employees and was an international operation. Then in late 2004 I received a call from CenterPoint Energy and decided to do it all over again: the design, the implementation, the roll out. I've been very fortunate and extremely blessed to be recruited by companies to help implement and roll out a new ethics program, and received incredible support in the process. I enjoy what I do; it just makes coming to work fun.

4. Compared to other jobs, how would you describe financial treatment in this field?

I think it's going to be like any other field; it's going to depend on what a company is looking for. If a company is looking for an experienced individual—then obviously, the compensation will reflect what that person can bring to the table. If a company is under a court mandate to implement an ethics program and they're bringing in attorneys to oversee this program, they're going to come in at a pretty healthy salary. On the other hand, if an individual wants to move into an ethics role with no experience, there will more than likely be some compensation considerations. Somebody looking at it today will find it fairly comparable to any other field, particularly if they have tenure and experience in HR, in Legal, or in Internal Audit.

That being said, people going into the ethics world today have had the strongest support regarding compensation we've ever had because of all the new legislation that has come out in the last few years. It's not viewed by Corporate America as, "Oh, it's just one of those soft, feel good departments. It's a non-revenue-producing department, so we'll base the salary range on that factor." Any more, if it's publicly traded, a company must have an ethics program. If a company has had problems that landed them on the front page of the Wall Street Journal – they have to have an ethics program. The investment community demands to see a visible and active program. There's so much consideration by companies, and budget & audit committees. Boards are saying, "Hey, we want this. We need this."

5. How would you describe job security in the field? Do you think there is a lot of mobility required?

Job security is here for a while. I don't see SOX going away any time soon; I don't see the New York Stock Exchange and the SEC changing their listing requirements any time soon. There should be no reservations on anyone's part who's looking at going into the ethics and compliance arena that it's one of those flavor of the month departments that's here today and gone tomorrow. Definitely, it's here. It's been here for a long time. Even before the Federal Sentencing Guidelines in the early 90s, there were companies out there that had the vision, and the desire to have ethics departments. In Corporate America and certainly even internationally, more and more companies are looking at implementing ethics departments. So for many of these companies that don't necessarily fall under a mandate or requirement that they must have a program—such as in countries in Europe, where it's not required—ultimately it's good for the bottom line of the company. It's a rewarding job, one that you can really feel good about. And it's not to say you don't have your challenges, not to say you don't have your frustrations. But without question, it's by far one of the most rewarding careers that someone can go into.

6. What field would you compare this field most closely to?

Probably HR and Legal—because of SOX and because of the new Federal Sentencing Guidelines revisions, we have all of the new legislation that has come into play. So there's certainly a stronger legal influence today in the ethics departments than there was historically, prior to the collapse of Enron or WorldCom or Tyco or some of the others. I do think someone that comes into the field with a strong HR background or has a Labor Relations background has a leg up. Now, granted, it may be just a very short leg, but they do have a bit of a leg up. Once you get into the ethics field, there's so much support from your fellow ethics officers that if you have an interest and a desire to learn, you can quickly get up to speed. Ninety percent—and this is a fairly recognized, benchmarked figure—ninety percent of the issues that come into an ethics department are HR-related. For that reason, I would continue to say that someone who has HR or Employee/Labor Relations knowledge or background definitely has a little bit of a leg up there.

7. What educational background do you recommend for those interested in getting into this field?

Well, of course, you can get your degree in all the various types of HR-related hats now. Some legal education or work experience would help, and even accounting and auditing. More and more, auditing departments today have sole responsibility, or ethics is aligned very closely with the internal audit department. Certainly, more and more of the reports that I prepare today are for board meetings and the Audit Committee. But a little smattering of all would help.

Several times a year, I am invited to various universities and have been doing this now for the last four or five years. It's interesting for me to see that ethics courses are now required as part of a student's curriculum. It used to be, if you were taking a business law course, there might be one page in one chapter where you might find the word "ethics" mentioned. That's no longer the case. Today, ethics courses are required for law students; there're numerous business law courses where ethics is required for the business and accounting majors. To me, that's really gratifying to see at the universities, because these young people are our business leaders of tomorrow.

8. What work experience would you recommend? If someone wants to get into the field, should they start somewhere else or try to go straight in?

I'm not saying it's insurmountable to go into an ethics department if you don't have any experience at all in that field, but it's not uncommon for companies that are implementing an ethics department to select people that have had a visible face in that company. They are known as individuals that are trustworthy, that people respect and will take their concerns to. So, I don't think that you have to come in with five years of experience necessarily to go into the ethics world, but typically, if it's going to be a new hire and not an internal transition, companies are looking for someone that has experience.

If someone is out there, and wants to get involved in the world of ethics, the best way to do it is to try to get on with a company and start out handling some of the calls for case intake. That provides you a really broad feel and understanding of what the employees' issues and concerns are. So many of the issues and concerns that are called into the helpline here at CenterPoint Energy or at a company elsewhere—Houston, Boston, New York, Los Angeles, Chicago, wherever—tend to be some of the same issues.

So for somebody just starting out, they could start out as "case managers": responsible for the intake of cases, ensuring they were accurately recorded and assigned for investigation. So if somebody comes into this world of ethics with no HR or employee relations experience, it gives them a great advantage to see what the steps and procedures were for conducting an investigation. They see the resolution, and what policy or law was violated, and what form of disciplinary action was taken if any.

9. Are there any books, articles that you think are good resources?

ethikos is one of the great periodicals that has come out. It's written so that you don't even have to be an ethics officer—certainly that's the bulk of the subscribers, but anybody could pick up an *ethikos* and learn from it.

One of the best books on ethics is called *The Ethical Edge*. It's unfortunately no longer in print and those of us who are fortunate enough to have a copy hold on to it like paper gold. It was written a number of years ago by Drs. Mike Hoffman, Ed Petry and Dawn-Marie Driscoll, and it takes 10-12 companies and talks about how they got to that ethical edge. What were some of the problems, what put them on the front page of the newspapers before the Enrons or the Worldcoms or some of the others that all roll off of our tongues now? That is still one of my favorites.

10. What would you say is the most gratifying part of working in this field?
Is there a more professional way to say, "Just knowing that you've helped individuals"? And you've helped your company, too. Really, it's just interacting with people and knowing that you've helped.

11. What is the most frustrating part of working in the field?
It's the challenge that some people choose not to listen, don't listen, and don't believe that the rules are applicable to them. We would be naïve to think that everybody "gets it." There's the challenge of trying to deliver the message so that people understand that not only is business ethics a good thing to do, not only is business ethics the right thing to do, but adhering to the rules of the road is something everybody has to do.

Do companies have an ethics program because it's the law today? I think to a certain degree, yes. It's also important that you have ethics programs because it's the right thing to do. There's a balance to be achieved. The trick of the balance, and the challenge of the balance, is to develop your program and incorporate a company's values; as well as the rules, the laws, and the policies. Because there are rules, there are laws, and there are policies, and they're in every company for a real reason.

12. What do you see as the opportunities for advancement in your area, such as for chief ethics officers? Where do you see potential growth in this field?
I certainly think ethics departments have more visibility today. It used to be, and still is to a large degree, if you had two minutes at the annual board meeting, or one board meeting annually, that was a lot of face time. Today, we're doing more and more with our boards, on a quarterly basis, providing more and more information to the audit committee. I laughingly say there was a time when many board members just wanted to know what time it was. Today, they are expected and want to know just how the clock works. Today most companies roll out additional ethics training to their respective boards as recommended by the Federal Sentencing Guidelines. So I think that the whole world, for the ethics officer, is broadening. What I might compare it to is, years ago, Human Resources was referred to as the personnel department, and they were the "keeper of personnel files," and that was it. Look at HR today! Now,

any company of any substance or size simply could not exist without a really strong Human Resources department, and they do so much more than just keep personnel files.

I see the same trend within the ethics departments. When I first got into it, there was maintaining the helpline database and being involved with code of conduct training, and all of a sudden we're finding ourselves in the board-room, and not just for two minutes once a quarter. We're finding ourselves in the boardroom more and more frequently, and we're working very closely with our outside auditors. So the whole dynamics of the ethics office, as well as the whole dynamics of the ethics officer, is growing by leaps and bounds. For some-one who is comfortable talking with the worker bees in the company, with the "you and me's" in the company, as well as in the boardroom, this is a wonderful job to have. But you have to be comfortable talking at all those levels, and you have to have a real feel for people.

13. When you made the move from Waste to CenterPoint, did your previous experience in compliance give you a better idea of what sorts of things to discuss with the employer? Did you talk about things like money or whether you were going to have membership in EOA, etc?

Absolutely, professional organizations offer opportunities to exchange ideas, program development plans and strategies. That was a huge factor for me. The opportunity to network and share valuable information which helps with your own program development is what helps most of us to have real, effective and meaningful programs. Otherwise, a company is susceptible to just having a paper or a title program. If you don't have some close associations with some of the organizations such as EOA, then you lose that opportunity to benchmark and see what best practices are going on out there. For me, it took on an addi-tional level of concern because I had been nominated to the board of the EOA. So that became a concern of mine, and once I met with the folks here and told them I had been nominated to EOA, they were incredibly supportive. Our Gen-eral Counsel and our CEO told me up front that CenterPoint Energy would be delighted with the prospect of having the ethics officer on the board and would support me in whatever way they could. And they have.

Was money a big issue for me? No, it wasn't. Waste had gone through some organizational and management changes and tied their ethics program in with another very meaningful program, but I guess I'm from the old school, and I still think that ethics should be a stand-alone initiative. At CenterPoint Energy, a great deal of attention and respect is given to ethics and compliance. I can't say enough about the importance Senior Management gives our program or my office. And they assured me there were no plans to merge ethics with anything else. So that was a big factor for me.

14. What are the other mistakes to avoid when you are getting into this field? Would you say that maybe arrogance or pride is a main one? Are there maybe little things?

That's well said. Someone should not come into a high level ethics position and say, "Well, I have been in the Legal Department," or "I was Director of Internal Audit," or "because I was head of HR, this is the way we're going to do it." Ethics departments are different. Frank Daly, former Ethics Officer for Northrup Grumman once said, "Ethics is a merging of values and laws." You have to be able to understand the importance of both concepts. The numbers, the monitoring—all of this is very important within an ethics department. So is trust and so is being able to communicate with someone, and not just dictate. It's more than just numbers; it may be what you're reporting, but there're relationships behind those numbers. There are real concerns and there are real issues behind those numbers. If all you can do is report the numbers, and not understand the concerns, you might be very successful, as a numbers person, but you're not going to be successful as an ethics officer.

15. Do you have any last thoughts?

Maybe I should come up with some wonderful something or other to end with, but it would just be cliché. So let me just say, it's a rewarding field, it's challenging; it's unlike any other profession I've been involved with, whether it was customer service or HR. It's unbelievably rewarding and gratifying both personally and professionally. The sharing of information between ethics officers is unlike anything I've ever seen or experienced before. And some of the relationships I've made with my counterparts are lasting and go beyond job descriptions and retirement. You typically don't see those types of business relationships/friendships that are sustained. Between ethics officers, it becomes more than just a handshake.

Being an ethics officer has really become a profession today. I can well remember in 1996, there were less than 300 members in the EOA, and I remember being at a meeting, and somebody talking about rotating out of an ethics officer position because of burnout. It is really interesting that today there are people who are trying to move into the ethics officer arena, or there are individuals who are choosing to leave companies because their job description has changed. Which mine did, and I elected to leave a very good company, which I still have a good relationship with, because I saw the focus shifting somewhat. So instead of ethics officers becoming burned out, quite the opposite has happened. We are very excited about what we do, and we don't want to leave it.

Interviewed September 6, 2005

When we first spoke with Linda, she was the Director of Corporate Ethics for Waste Management in Houston. Prior to publication, we learned Linda was with a new company and the interview was updated accordingly.

Richard Gruner

Law Professor

1. What is your current role: i.e., title, employer, and city where you work?

I'm a professor of law at the Whittier Law School in Costa Mesa, California.

2. Now, is compliance an explicit part of your role at Whittier, or is it instead an interest you hold personally?

It comes up in two contexts in my role as a law professor. I do a substantial amount of research and teaching in this area, particularly in the context of Continuing Education programs and scholarly research articles that I write about the standards governing compliance, as well as some discussion of techniques relevant to compliance programs. So one setting where it affects my work is in a research context. The other is that I do teach courses on white-collar and corporate crime in which I discuss the impact of compliance programs and the developing standards governing compliance techniques.

3. Is there anything else that you do relevant to the field in your job? Do you interact with other people dealing in the field?

I have been involved with, first of all, the advisory group for the Organizational Sentencing Guidelines, which was active over an 18 month period ending in the fall of 2003, in which we gave advice and recommendations to the U.S. Sentencing Commission on corporate compliance program standards. And in that process, both within the advisory group and in connection with hearings that we held, I was in contact with a wide variety of compliance-related experts and gathered a lot of very useful insights from them about what the current criteria for an effective compliance program should include. And then another context in which I have been interacting with other compliance experts is that I've been working with a group called OCEG (Open Compliance and Ethics Group), which is also developing a set of privately-developed standards or guidelines for compliance related programs.

4. How did you first become interested in compliance and organizational ethics, what drew you to it, and how long ago was that?

My original exposure was actually as an inside corporate counsel with IBM; I was with IBM as a lawyer from 1978 to '83. And while I was at IBM, I worked particularly with anti-employment discrimination compliance programs, which IBM had instituted at that time and was really very effective in pursuing. I had the luck of working with one of their senior lawyers, who was in charge of overseeing those kinds of anti-discrimination programs. And so I learned from him, and from the work that we did, a lot about the merits of systematic compliance efforts. I more recently generalized that knowledge into other compliance areas.

5. **Has a focus/specialty in compliance and ethics factored at all into your own financial standing? As for people who are interested in getting into the field, would taking courses in compliance and ethics be a good financial move, or is that more something that would depend on the job they chose?**

Well, let me answer that at two different levels, one of those my own experience, and that through a legal education. I have not, since I stopped being an IBM lawyer in '83, actually been in a practice setting where I was dealing with compliance processes. I would say as an academic, it's been a booming field, and this has certainly been helpful in pursuing the compliance field as it has gained importance and notoriety in both business and legal settings. But my perspective is as an academic, and I'm not sure that translates directly to financial success. Having said that though, as a legal educator, this is certainly a field where there are many opportunities for lawyers or persons with legal training to prosper and gain employment, because the compliance effort and performance of companies is recognized now as a critical area. And I think we'll see it increasingly so recognized, such that there are going to be many different opportunities related to compliance. So in that respect, as an educator I can see this as a prospering area that certainly ought to be a good career path.

6. **Do you think that in this field any financial compensation considerations are dependent on the public attention or the big scandals that happen, or do you think that it is pretty stable at this point?**

No, it's definitely still a growth field and will be probably for the next decade. To a certain extent, it was driven somewhat by the scandals. It's also driven though by developments such as the Federal Sentencing reforms that have been initiated as far back as 1984, when Congress passed major sentencing legislation which increased the types of penalties that were threatened against companies and their executives. And with those increased penalties, companies have increasingly paid attention to these kinds of compliance matters; and of course the Sarbanes-Oxley Act created another major wave of new attention. So I would say it's not even primarily the public attention that's driving this; it's actual dollars and cents concern on the part of companies as they see what they're threatened with if they don't pick a more responsible and effective approach to compliance.

7. **Considering that it is a growing field right now, how is the job security in the field? You can also speak specifically about people who want to teach. Do they have to be able/willing to travel, to move to a different city to get work in this field?**

On the teaching side, the dynamics of it are similar to other law teaching fields and in that respect, to be frank, there aren't too many opportunities for a law teacher; it's a fairly small community. But that's not, I think, where most of the people with compliance-related training would be looking for employment anyway. For the lawyers with compliance training, the career paths are either as inside counsel or outside counsel (there are other jobs for persons of specialized managerial training, but I'm less familiar with their career paths). Both of which would be working with companies in setting up systematic compliance programs or responding to indications that their compliance programs are inadequate in some way and giving advice on how to improve them. And there's certainly a substantial, and I think still expanding number of jobs in those areas. I think, too, people who are already doing that work in corporate environments are seeing their status increase as the companies involved pay more attention to these kind of compliance issues.

8. **What field would you compare this field most closely to? What sorts of people would find it of interest? Also, how would teaching this subject compare to teaching other subjects? Are there many differences in theory and practice?**

Well, again, focusing on training lawyers to work with compliance issues, the fields that it relates to or would be parallel to would be other highly specialized, regulatory law bodies. Now that can be a wide range of things, including securities law requirements or tax requirements or government procurement requirements or retirement plan regulation requirements. So I would see it as parallel in that sense to these other detailed, regulatory bodies of law. And the teaching is comparable as well; as to be really well versed at these kinds of compliance standards and methods, there's a substantial body of standards and methodologies to study. And so it's hard to teach this in a complete manner; it would take a series of courses to really cover it.

9. **Is there anything that you might see in a student (personal traits, etc.) that would lead you to suggest they do more research on their own in compliance?**

Generally, one aspect that would be helpful, and I see it in some of my students, is existing managerial background in any business environment. So there's a notion that they have been involved in some sort of systematic management process, and then can take some of those insights into thinking about how compliance techniques would be incorporated into a business environment. They can then also think about how existing standards for compliance programs should be interpreted in light of the managerial's dynamics or the situation. That's not so much a personal trait as it is an element of background. To have a business background and even a moderate sense of being in a bigger corporate environment, seeing how the management processes work, that's very helpful in having them understand what's at stake in some of these compliance settings.

10. What is the most gratifying part of teaching compliance?

I view the compliance field as a chance to be positive, really at two different levels. One is that I really do believe that effective compliance programs prevent offenses, and thereby serve the public and serve the interests of the corporation involved. So in that sense a compliance-oriented practice can be a very positive, constructive practice, more so maybe than a lot of legal, where you're just trying to clean up somebody else's problem. The other is that the setting of corporate liabilities is a setting where corporations can distinguish themselves in a positive way. They can show that they are indeed responsible and forward looking and publicly oriented by taking an aggressive, preventative stance. So in that sense it's part of a corporate-level ethics that is very positive and which has gained increasing interest and concern in the last few years. So those aspects of both public service and particularly, corporate ethics and positive corporate action, are very positive sides of the compliance field.

11. What is frustrating about the field? What does not make sense or is very aggravating?

Well, there are three features. One is that there's a lingering doubt that even well constructed compliance programs mean anything. I just don't understand that cynicism; I believe that compliance programs are based on sound management principles, and if you believe that companies can be managed, then you believe that compliance can be managed. I find that criticism distressing—the notion that a lot of these programs are really window dressing and maybe they're all window dressing. So that's number one.

Number two is that it's distressing that more executives don't really themselves believe in the compliance and ethics biz; there are some that are giving it lip service rather than digging more deeply and viewing this as a management challenge that can be addressed through corporate management techniques. So it's distressing to see corporate executives themselves not believe too in a compliance context what they do believe in marketing or quality control or other more traditional management areas.

I guess the third point relates to a point that I was making earlier that in the educational field, from the business school side, there is first, not more attention both to the legal forces of corporate threats that managers ought to be attentive to, and second, the specific importance of compliance as a standard component of management training that all corporate managers at the level of MBA training should be at least exposed to.

12. On opportunities for advancement and potential growth, is there anything that you are aware of that could develop within the teaching side, or within law schools? Or are there options that might open up because of your interest in compliance? Do you think there will ever be a position for a compliance professor that you could take?

In one sense, those positions already exist, and they're occupied by people who are teaching in the white-collar crime field. There are a substantial number of those through law schools throughout the country. What I don't see is perhaps a greater emphasis on inside counsel practice, which would include more compliance-oriented training (but perhaps some other issues of particular interest to inside counsels). As a former inside counsel with IBM, I've over the years kept that perspective, and I've been disappointed that there hasn't been more law teaching aimed at people who will end up as inside counsels. Because I think it is a distinct, and in my experience, very positive type of practice. And so what I would hope there would be in the law teaching side of things is more course content, and perhaps more specialized professors who are teaching classes (on inside counsel practice) something comparable to what we do teach about litigation practice. And that kind of course would surely include a major set of treatments of compliance-related issues.

13. Is there anything that you would recommend to people, namely students or professors/colleagues, who are interested in getting into this field (or specifically, teaching the subject)?

Aiming at the students first, I would indicate that, as with many fields of legal practice, it pays to capitalize on as much of your pre-existing background—that is background existing as the student enters law school—as possible. If the person has particular background in procurement or the health care field or securities field, they might want to think about how to expand that into a compliance role in that field. So in a sense they'll have a leg up, based on their existing knowledge in terms of the dynamics in entering a compliance role in that same field. Once they pick a field that they might be interested in, in addition to whatever training they can get in compliance standards per se, training in parallel substantive law will be a major advantage. So for example, to be in a compliance role in the securities field, get as much treatment of securities regulation laws as possible (and now securities fraud related laws as well). As much training as they can get in those substantive areas will carry over into compliance roles.

Beyond that, the major source of the training at that kind of level tends to be in continuing education contexts. And actually, PLI puts on wonderful programs and has wonderful materials that are covering these kinds of issues at the next level, as they track what are the compliance techniques that are needed and what are the state of the art issues in crafting those. And so even at the law student level, I would encourage students to try to look at and even participate in some of these continuing education programs, if they can arrange that.

14. What educational background would you recommend? Would you recommend getting a legal background, or a business background, or even communications?

There are two different ways to come at it, and those lead maybe to two different roles. Legal training is probably the way to be most effective in the field, because there are legal issues at two different levels. One is "What does an adequate compliance program look like?" and that leads to a lot of legal standards; secondly, what are the aims of compliance programs? What kinds of offenses are you really trying to prevent? That often requires some legal training to understand as well. Having said that though, there is kind of a third perspective, or third dimension here beyond the compliance program law and the substantive area law, which is the management technique side. The features of a good compliance program are dictated by management principles. And so a background coming at compliance from a management function viewpoint is a valuable background as well. And when I say management function, someone who's dealt with quality control programs or has dealt with any other specific, specialized management programs usually translates the experience of what they've got into a valuable compliance function. Ideally in a company setting, there would be some mix of these types of people, somebody with extensive management experience, with maybe limited legal training, complemented by somebody else with substantial legal training but limited managerial experience. The two of them together would produce great compliance leadership. And obviously those two different kinds of leaders could well come from substantially different kinds of training background.

15. Theoretically speaking, if 10-15 years down the road, a business or a law school were to start offering a four-year compliance & ethics degree, do you think that that would be a good resource? Or do you think that it would be too separate from law and business, that it would not give you enough of the basic grounding that would be required?

Well, I have to think about that degree of separation. I think what we're headed for and what would be a valuable emphasis is for this to be viewed as a sub-function within business school training. In other words, as people perhaps specialize in business school in marketing or product design or even tax considerations these days, that they could specialize in compliance management considerations. So it would benefit from not being totally separate, but rather being seen as a subspecialty within business management.

16. Is there any work experience that you would recommend? When it comes to teaching would you suggest approaching a potential employer with a mind for introducing compliance and ethics courses, or should they move in to teach business and law broadly, and then suggest the other things?

Taking the law teaching side, which I'm much more familiar with, I don't know that a new teacher would be able to be engaged solely to do, or even primarily to do compliance-oriented teaching. It would have to be part of a broader package, and currently the new law teacher would probably want to emphasize that they're interested in, and hopefully have the background for, teaching white-collar crime courses, which would include a major treatment of compliance-oriented topics. But even with that, a typical new teacher's complement of courses would be say four different one-semester courses over the course of a year. So that would be perhaps one quarter of the package that a new professor might teach. So what I'm saying is, that would be part of what you'd want to present as a new teacher, but it would be helpful to have a broader set of either business or core legal courses that one was also interested in teaching. To me the compliance side is sort of an advanced flavoring for the complement of teaching the person is going to offer to a law school, but don't rely on that as the sole attractive feature that the new teacher is trying to present.

17. So what are the mistakes in approaching compliance? What sorts of attitudes or choices are going to make it more difficult to deal with the field?

There is some cynicism, I think, inside companies and outside. Such as the notion that even managers or operating employees think that the efforts being taken to implement and promote compliance programs are just window dressing and don't need to be paid attention to. The mistakes are in not trying as much as possible to dispel that, both in terms of messages from top executives, but also just follow-through. Companies now, particularly as they try to improve their programs, are at a stage where the biggest risk is not doing what they said they were going to do. And the first time there's some major incident or misconduct where there isn't a lot of discipline, reform and actual, visible response in accordance with the compliance program a company set up, the message is clear to the operating employees—"Well, that isn't really an important management function."

I think that line employees are actually pretty sophisticated in sorting out the real from the illusory, and the primary way they do it is to see what counts in actual, difficult corporate circumstances. The main thing that line employees look to in deciding what's real in a corporate environment is the question of, "What does the company do when put to the test?" In a corporate misconduct setting, that really is a question of "How does the company respond once it has the opportunity to do so?" And if the response is weak, then the message is clear to employees: compliance really isn't all that important.

18. Is there any book or other reading that you would recommend? Are there any texts you have used, whether dealing with compliance or white-collar crime?

Well, let me give you two answers. I recommend the two books that I mentioned of mine: *The Legal Audit*, originally authored by Lou Brown and Anne Kandel and now authored by the two of them plus me; and then *Corporate Criminal Liability and Prevention*, from Law Journal Press, of which I'm the sole author. Those are reference texts. The one book that I have used for teaching is called *Corporate and White Collar Crime: Cases and Materials*, by a professor at Washington University of St. Louis by the name of Kathleen Brickey. That is a longstanding corporate and white-collar crime casebook, and it's quite good. It's particularly attractive to me in that it does more with the corporate type of liabilities than do many of the white-collar crime texts.

19. Do you have any final comments on careers in the field, for those looking at academia, or otherwise?

I think that as the interest in compliance programs and controls—those controls at issue now under Sarbanes-Oxley—as those kind of concerns continue to increase, there's going to be an expanding field, with both a need for specialized personnel and also for new thinking. In fact, this is still somewhat of a pioneering area in an expanding field, and that has to be good in a career, as well as public-policy, sense. So I think it would be both a setting where people would find the jobs available and also find the jobs to be interesting once they got into them, because it's really establishing an important new sub-domain.

Interviewed June 6, 2005

9   What Training and Certifications Are Available for Compliance Professionals?

What subjects should compliance professionals study?

Because compliance and ethics is still a relatively new field, there is not a great deal of established training and education designed for the compliance professional. Later in this chapter we will survey what is currently available. But first we will provide some guidance on what compliance professionals need to know to do this difficult job.

One of the threshold questions is whether those interested in entering the field or already in this line of work should pursue training as opposed to learning on the job. We believe that on-the-job, real-world experience is important for this field. This is certainly where we learn our most valuable lessons and practice tips. However, this should not take away from the value of studying in the classroom context. While the best adult learning is based on experience, an organized classroom approach can assure broader scope of coverage, including points that may be missed in the workplace.

This point is, of course, not unique to compliance. Practitioners in many fields would say the same thing: their most important learning happened in the real world. There is nevertheless an important role for training and education. For example, on-the-job training will teach us much about the specific people and company we work with; on the other hand, we may miss alternative ways to approach problems. We may know everything about how a problem has challenged our industry, but not realize that practitioners in other industries have developed a much more effective technique that never occurred to us. We may understand the nuts and bolts of daily work, but be missing the broader trends that would tell us what to expect around the corner.

Moreover, it is not of much help to students still in school to tell them to learn about compliance on the job. This argument is just too circular to be useful, since those making hiring decisions want someone who brings something useful to the table. If a company is hiring a compliance officer, obviously experience will be necessary, but this is true of any officer position in any company. On the other hand, as the field has expanded, opportunities have opened up at entry-level positions as well. If someone is going to spend time in school, why not use the time to learn valuable lessons about the field? And certainly those already in compliance positions, if they want to keep their options open for possibly changing jobs in this field, can gain from learning about the many different aspects of the compliance and ethics world.

What should a compliance and ethics person learn? In Appendix 9A we have provided a model curriculum as an ideal for the compliance person. Some of these topics may be available in existing courses and training programs, while others, such as the survey of legal risk areas, should be covered in the university context but are not offered yet. In the short term this curriculum can provide a useful checklist for those looking for useful course topics. In the longer term we hope to see a more organized approach to training in this area that will include more of these topics.

What is available from the universities: business schools and other programs

At this point we are not aware of any degree program focused on the broad range of corporate compliance. (The Australasian Compliance Institute has reached a similar conclusion, reporting on its Website that "as yet there are no Undergraduate degrees and only a few Masters courses. ACI is working with several universities to develop qualifications that align with our Professional Accreditation requirements.") However, in the health care compliance field, Quinnipiac University offers a six-course certificate program in health care compliance that has been certified by the Health Care Compliance Association. The program is jointly offered by the School of Business and the School of Law to provide the "foundation and the skills to successfully implement the administrative and management principles required to function as competent and knowledgeable health care compliance professionals."

In its first year, the program is restricted to students already enrolled in graduate programs in the university. Thereafter it is to be open to those with a bachelor's degree and five or more years of experience, or attorneys seeking to specialize in health care compliance.

According to the school's Website[1], the courses in the sixteen-credit program will cover: "the principles and specifics of health care compliance; principles of general management; legal aspects of health care compliance; and the principles of financial management/auditing." Upon completion certificate holders will be eligible to take the HCCA national certifying examination.

It is expected that other schools will offer similar programs in the health care compliance field. Perhaps development of a national certification program in the broader field of compliance and ethics could lead to similar educational offerings, but thus far there is no degree program in this field.

What is available from the law schools

In what is reported to be the first full law school course on corporate compliance, Professor Paul McGreal has developed a full semester corporate compliance course at the South Texas College of Law.[2] The course gives a survey of the field, teaches practical compliance skills such as drafting and interviewing, and requires a seminar paper. The first part of the course introduces students to the basics of the field. Next, they are introduced to a specific risk area, in this case FCPA, so that they can apply their learning in a focused way. The third part of the course involves applying what they learn in the various compliance tasks.

The topics covered in the course, by week, are:

Week 1:   Introduction: What is compliance?
Week 2:   Review of vicarious liability
Week 3:   Why have an ethics and compliance program?
Week 4:   Introduction to the FCPA
Week 5:   Risk assessment
Week 6:   Role of the board
Week 7:   Structuring the compliance function
Week 8:   Code of conduct
Week 9:   Drafting compliance policies
Week 10: Training
Week 11: Monitoring, auditing, and evaluating the compliance program
Week 12: Enforcement and discipline
Week 13: Corporate culture

In addition to the program at South Texas, there have been efforts to include some coverage of compliance and ethics in other law school courses. Appendix 9B contains an outline of a presentation and exercise on this topic that is used in a corporate counseling class at the University of Pennsylvania Law School. The compliance coverage is limited to one two-hour segment. A similar approach had been used in a course on corporate counseling that had been presented by corporate lawyers at Rutgers University's Law School in Camden, New Jersey.

Beyond these instances, it is likely to be a difficult road for those seeking more than a cursory approach to this subject in the law schools. Although the subject of business and organizational misconduct has enormous social and political significance, there is still quite some distance to travel before the academic institutions catch up to the development of this field.

Training and certification from the compliance membership organizations

In the absence of assistance from academia, the membership organizations have been a consistent source for education and training in compliance and ethics. Their efforts fall into three categories. The first includes membership conferences and meetings. These are typically conventional presentations on topics of interest to practitioners. The second is the academy or course approach. These are typically limited in the number of attendees and are more formal courses. The third offering is the certification program. These typically require completion of certain levels of training, experience in the field, successful completion of an examination, and adherence to an ethical code.

Ethics and Compliance Officer Association (ECOA)[3]

ECOA, formerly EOA, holds two major events annually with presenters on a variety of topics. One of these meetings is relatively open ("Annual Business Ethics & Compliance Conference"), and the second is limited to the ECOA's Sponsoring Partners ("Sponsoring Partners Forum").

ECOA also co-sponsors, with the Center for Business Ethics at Bentley College, a week-long course called Managing Ethics in Organizations. As stated in the Website, "Attendees explore the complexities and nuances of their work. A typical session may include a short presentation, a case study with a role-play and a question and answer period." This program covers knowledge and skills needed for the in-house practitioner. Segments include ethics and the law, conducting effective investigations, training and globalization. While some ECOA services are available only to members, and members do get a discount for this course, Managing Ethics in Organizations is open to anyone who is interested.

Society of Corporate Compliance and Ethics (SCCE)[4]

SCCE offers all three types of educational programs. The first is an annual meeting that offers speakers and discussion across the range of compliance and ethics topics. The second is a series of workshops held around the country. These smaller sessions allow more focused discussion on specific compliance topics. Lastly, in 2006, the organization established a professional certification program for compliance and ethics professionals in all industries. The Certified Compliance and Ethics Professional (CCEP) program provides for the first time a national standard of requisite knowledge for the profession. As such, earning the certification can help working professionals demonstrate individual knowledge and expertise. (For more background on CCEP certification, see Appendix 9C: "Certified Compliance & Ethics Professional (CCEP) Program Overview.") A newly established Academy will provide practical training in a four-day program that will also prepare candidates for the certification exam.

Health Care Compliance Association (HCCA)[5]

HCCA's approach covers all three training elements: a variety of programs, structured academies, and a certification program. HCCA's general Academy, recommended for those who have not had much prior compliance education, provides practical training on all aspects of health care compliance and is also intended to provide sufficient grounding for those seeking certification. The Advanced Academy is designed for advanced level compliance professionals, and is taught at a college level, with instructors structuring the course around the participants' educational and professional backgrounds. HCCA also offers numerous programs throughout the year, as well as its major annual conference. HCCA's local chapters also offer programs.

The Health Care Compliance Certification Board (HCCB), which was created by HCCA but operates independently, administers a certification program for those in health care compliance. Certification requires initial and ongoing training, adherence to the HCCA ethical code, and successful completion of an exam. Those who qualify receive the designation "Certified in Healthcare Compliance" (CHC). As of October 2006 at least 1,030 professionals have been certified, and the HCCB is developing a more advanced phase of certification.

Australasian Compliance Institute (ACI)[6]

Like SCCE and HCCA, ACI provides both training and certification. It holds a major annual convention, as well as more focused programs during each year. The approach is described on the ACI Website:

> "ACI has a structured Accreditation program that provides the
> core compliance training for both those entering the profes-
> sion and for the more advanced professional. We also have a

range of courses and materials available for those interested in compliance as a profession, or those who have compliance responsibilities as part of their role responsibilities."

Anyone can take the courses, but only members of ACI are eligible for accreditation. There are three levels of accreditation based on the levels of difficulty.

Defense Industry Initiative on Business Ethics and Conduct (DII)[7]

DII is an organization of major U.S. defense contractors committed to applying ethical business practices. The group sponsors an annual best practices forum in Washington, D.C., that provides background and coverage of compliance initiatives in this industry.

International Ombudsman Association (IOA)[8]

IOA sponsors Ombudsman 101 (among other programs), which includes coverage on confidentiality, how to establish and run an ombuds office, and how to gather data.

Compliance Institute (UK)[9]/International Compliance Association[10]

These two compliance organizations based in the UK offer a Foundation Certificate in Compliance Practice in the financial services and money laundering areas. The program is intended for those new to the field or who need refresher training. The program is expected to take six to nine months to complete, involving daytime workshops as well as distance learning.

Other providers

In addition to the universities and membership organizations, there are other groups that cover education and training. The Practising Law Institute (PLI)[11] offers programs for lawyers on compliance programs. The Conference Board[12] hosts an annual conference on business ethics in New York. A variety of bar groups, including the Association of Corporate Counsel[13], the American Bar Association (ABA)[14] and local bar groups offer programs for lawyers similar to the PLI approach.

For those with more of an ethics orientation, some of the ethics centers offer training and seminars. For further discussion of ethics centers, see Appendix E. There are also for-profit groups that provide training. The American Conference Institute,[15] for example, offers a program on the FCPA which includes coverage of compliance programs in that risk area.

Appendix 9A

Model Curriculum

I. Compliance and Business Ethics: What you need to know

This first category covers subjects in the compliance/ethics field that you need to know, or that are useful for practitioners.

A. History and threshold considerations

1. **What is the field**: explains what the field is about and how it differs from other subjects. Describes the subject areas and functions that are part of compliance.

2. **History of compliance**: provides the background and context of compliance and ethics programs.

3. **Who are the players in this field**: explains the various organizations in the compliance and ethics field, including the membership organizations, relevant government agencies, and providers in the compliance and ethics industry.

4. **What information sources are available**: describes the available sources for additional information about the field.

5. **What are the professional standards for this field**

   a. **Lawyers and other professions**: how do the ethical standards for these professions relate to compliance work; are there conflicts?

   b. **Compliance/ethics organizations' standards**: SCCE, IOA, HCCA, ECOA, ACI: what are these organizations' ethical standards? How do they affect the compliance and ethics professional's performance and activities?

B. What are the standards for compliance programs: considers the expectations for compliance programs.

1. **The basics of the Sentencing Guidelines standards**: covers all the elements of the Guidelines generally. The details are in the how-to discussion.

2. **What are the other compliance program standards**

   a. **US: SOX, NYSE, Kolstad/Ellerth, DOJ, OIG, etc.**: covers all these compliance standards and explains the differences compared to the Sentencing Guidelines. Covers government policy statements regarding what should be in a compliance program.

   b. **Global**: at this point, just reference the fact that there are also standards outside the US, but these are covered in a later portion of the training dealing with global compliance.

C. The "how to" of compliance programs

1. **The ins and outs of risk assessment**: explains the scope of risk assessment and the need to weigh the likelihood of a violation and its potential impact. Covers legal, ethical and reputational risks.

2. **The ABC's of codes of conduct**: discusses why these are considered so important, what they cover, and what the techniques are that make them effective. Also covers other types of company policies.

3. **Establishing the program's infrastructure**: covers all aspects of Sentencing Guidelines element number 2; what is a compliance officer, what is the role of subject matter experts, and why there needs to be compliance personnel in all of the business units. What is the role of a compliance committee? Addresses how to strengthen the position of the compliance staff so they have sufficient clout to get the job done.

4. **The board of directors' roles and responsibilities**: boards have taken on an increased role in compliance after Caremark and the Enron series of cases. This covers what their diligence needs to entail, and the need for regular reporting on the progress and effectiveness of the compliance program. This also discusses what board training is appropriate under Sentencing Guidelines element 4, and the application of company codes of conduct to board members (now required under the NYSE listing rules). Includes the value of a strong board of directors' resolution and audit committee charter.

5. **Background checks and compliance due diligence**: provides guidance on how to conduct background checks, how to avoid promoting the wrong people, and how to handle such due diligence without violating anti-discrimination laws. Also covers conducting due diligence on compliance programs in acquisitions.

6. **Training and communications**: what is effective for adults, what are the best practices, and how should a company mix effective live training with online techniques. Also covers the use of Websites for communications. What have been the most successful means of reaching employees with the compliance message?

7. **The ins and outs of auditing, deep dives and other checking tools**: explains how the Sentencing Guidelines require auditing and monitoring that can detect criminal conduct, and delves into the range of techniques

that can be used to meet the standards of Sentencing Guidelines element 5. Covers the issue of auditor independence and professionalism.

8. **Helplines, ombuds, whistleblowers and retaliation: What you need to know:** explains the requirements of Guidelines element 5 and the provisions of Sarbanes-Oxley dealing with reporting systems and whistle blowing. Reviews the legal protections provided for whistleblowers, and how to prevent retaliation. Delves into the role of the ombudsman and how they differ from other compliance people.

9. **Discipline, evaluation and incentives:** addresses the meaning of Sentencing Guidelines element 6, including ways to ensure that discipline is effective and reaches managers who failed to take preventive steps. Also explores the role of incentives in compliance and ethics programs, and how personnel evaluation systems can be tailored to promote the compliance program.

10. **Measurement techniques in compliance programs:** explains the meaning of the Sentencing Guidelines reference to evaluating a program's effectiveness. Discusses the techniques that can be used for this purpose, including surveys, focus groups, deep dives, audits, and testing techniques.

11. **Surveys and focus groups:** moves from the general discussion of measurement to the detailed aspects of conducting effective surveys and focus groups. What are the do's and don'ts in conducting surveys; how do you get employees to open up in focus groups.

12. **How to conduct investigations:** under the Sentencing Guidelines element 7, how a company responds to wrongdoing is a crucial point. This coverage goes into the details of conducting effective interviews, how to examine paper and electronic records, how to provide reports, and how to conduct root cause analyses after the investigation is completed. What are the standards that should apply for investigations?

13. **Documenting your program:** for programs to be credible, there must be sufficient documentation to show that the program really happened. The compliance office itself must also adhere to document retention requirements, including those imposed in litigation and government investigations.

14. **Crisis management in the compliance context:** explains why the compliance office must be prepared for the worst case, how to draft a useful crisis management plan, and what to do in an actual compliance crisis.

15. **Industry practices:** how to determine industry practice and make the most of industry practice groups; how to form and manage such groups.

16. **Dealing with agents, vendors and other third parties**: the Sentencing Guidelines make several references to agents or other third parties, and companies face substantial compliance risks from the acts of third parties. This coverage deals with what those risks are and how to deal with them without actually increasing the company's own risks. What is the appropriate due diligence in retaining agents, consultants and other third parties?

D. **Globalization of compliance programs**
   1. **Taking a program outside your own country**: how does a company in one country take its compliance program overseas? If a company operates around the world, what adjustments need to be made for the different cultures and legal systems? What happens when different countries' laws conflict?
   2. **International compliance standards:** other countries have developed standards for compliance programs, e.g., Australia, Canada, Italy, South Africa, the ISO standards for environmental programs. What are these standards and how do they differ from the Sentencing Guidelines elements? How can a compliance office be sure it is current on all the evolving compliance program standards, including those in risk areas like privacy and environment?
   3. **A global trend**: explains why the development of compliance programs is a global trend, following the growth in global enforcement actions against corporate violations.

E. **Dealing with the government, litigation and the legal system**
   1. **The legal risks of compliance programs**: delves into all the ways a compliance program can go wrong and actually increase a company's compliance and legal risks. Also discusses the legal risks faced by compliance people and how to minimize those risks. Includes potential conflicts with labor law, privacy protections, and anti-discrimination laws.
   2. **How to work with lawyers**: lawyers play a key role in the legal system and in keeping a company within the law. How is the lawyer's role different from the compliance professional's? How can compliance and legal work together without friction?
   3. **Dealing with litigation and privileges**: compliance programs need to be designed and operated with litigation in mind. What are the risks for compliance programs from litigation and how can a company miti-

gate those risks? What are the privilege and related protections that are available; what are their limitations and how can they best be used in the compliance program? What causes waiver of privilege protection?

4. **How to be an effective witness**: with the potential for litigation in mind, what does a compliance person need to know about the litigation process? How should a compliance person prepare for a deposition? For testimony in a trial? What is involved in preparing a written affidavit?

5. **Presenting your program to the government**: this is a practice exercise in which the compliance person actually presents a compliance program to a team playing the role of a government enforcement unit. The compliance person learns the importance of preparation and how to motivate others to be prepared for this eventuality. The compliance person also learns the importance of keeping an ongoing presentation binder that tells the compliance program's full story.

F. **Business ethics**

1. **Its history and substance**: how does business ethics relate to compliance and ethics? What is the history of business ethics in academia and the business world? What are the different approaches to this subject? What is the difference between law and ethics?

2. **The ethical decision-making model**: understanding how to deal with ethical issues; providing employees with tools to deal with issues, even when there are no direct answers in the law.

3. **The wasted debate: "ethics vs. compliance"**: discusses the debate between ethics and compliance or law and values; what are the weaknesses on each side of this debate? Examines alternatives to taking sides in this debate.

G. **Key legal risk areas: a survey review and related red flags.** Covers the basic elements of the law and the risks in each of these areas. Also enumerates the red flags that indicate heightened risk. These are especially important in audits, focus groups, deep dives and investigations. No short course could cover these to the same depth that a lawyer would master, but such an overview course can familiarize the compliance person with key risk areas. This better enables the compliance person to know when to consult legal counsel.

1. **Harassment**: covers protections of the various societal groups and types of conduct that are off limits.

2. **Discrimination**: covers the protections of the various groups and the

types of employment decisions that would trigger these laws.

3. **Antitrust**: deals with laws protecting competition, including prohibitions against conspiracies, monopolistic practices, price discrimination, and business torts.

4. **Conflicts/gifts/bribery**: companies address gifts and conflicts both to prevent illegal conduct and to avoid having employees make decisions not in the company's interests. Explores the legal risks of gift giving and conflicts, as well as industry practice in dealing with this area.

5. **International legal risks**: this subject deals with extra-territorial application of US law, including export control, trade restrictions, anti-terrorism rules and the Anti-boycott Act.

6. **FCPA and overseas bribery laws**: what are the requirements of the US FCPA and how do they compare to similar laws adopted by other OECD countries? What are facilitating payments and who is a foreign official? What are the classic red flags for bribery?

7. **Intellectual property**: this coverage includes the law on trademarks, patents, trade secrets, and copyright. Copyright coverage includes printed and electronic materials and the fair use doctrine. Trade secret protection includes the Economic Espionage Act.

8. **Responding to the government**: what does a company need to know when it receives a subpoena from the government? What should employees do in response to a search warrant? What are the responsibilities for retaining records once a government investigation starts?

9. **Accounting fraud/earnings management**: when do accounting practices cross the line into accounting fraud? What are the red flags that may appear even in field operations?

10. **Retaliation**: what are the various laws prohibiting retaliation? What is required under Sarbanes Oxley in the US and the UK's whistleblower protection statute?

11. **Environmental, health and safety**: explains the key laws prohibiting air, water and land pollution, and the right-to-know laws. What are the common risk areas that apply even to non-manufacturing companies? What are the most important workplace safety requirements?

12. **Insider trading**: what are the restrictions on insider trading? What are the limits on tipping others? What are the restrictions on short-swing profits?

13. **Privacy:** what must companies do to protect customer/consumer privacy? How must employee records be protected? To whom does HIPAA

apply? Why do companies outside the EU have to worry about the privacy directive? Which countries impose privacy compliance program requirements?

14. **Sarbanes-Oxley**: what are the compliance obligations imposed by SOX? Does section 404 really require everything the accountants say it does? Are all the provisions of SOX restricted to publicly-traded companies?

15. **Consumer protection**: any company that deals with the public needs to understand the legal protections for consumers. What are the restrictions on consumer advertising? What is the relationship of the FTC Act and state consumer protection laws? What differences might you see in other countries, e.g., for advertising to children?

16. **Mandatory compliance programs**: one of the more recent developments in the compliance field is a shift to legally required compliance program elements. These range from mandatory sexual harassment training in some US states, to Canadian laws requiring privacy compliance programs, to programs dictated under government settlement agreements. Failure to implement these steps is itself a legal violation.

17. **Penalties, damages & other remedies**: explores the full range of remedies available to the government, private plaintiffs and the courts in dealing with company wrongdoing. Discusses criminal penalties, treble damages, civil penalties, punitive damages, imposition of counsel fees, debarment and private damages. Also explains probation, consent decrees, corporate integrity agreements (CIAs), and deferred prosecution agreements.

18. **Other:** the points above are important ones for most companies, but there are many areas of legal and ethical concern. Any regulated industry needs to understand its regulators and their requirements, such as the FDA for the pharmaceutical industry, and HHS for healthcare.

H. Case studies

1. **Enron**: those learning compliance/ethics should understand what happened in cases like Enron's, and what could have been done to prevent such compliance debacles. Discussion includes determining what compliance steps could make a difference in cases like this. Enron is just one example, but has the advantage of having been extensively investigated with the results made public.

2. **WorldCom**: another example comparable to Enron.

3. **Parmalat**: of the many cases in the Enron Era, Parmalat is particularly

useful to study, because it occurred in Italy, not the US. This demonstrates the universal nature of the compliance issues.

4. **Others**: there are many examples of interesting cases to examine, but the most instructive are those with a substantial public record.

II. Personal and professional skills

These are topics not tied solely to compliance, but are important personal skills in this field and others.

A. **How to make effective presentations/public speaking**: this is an essential skill to be effective in the compliance field. Mastery of public speaking can lead to much more rapid advancement in this and other fields. Because this is skills training, the format includes actual presentations and critiquing of presenters.

B. **How to sell: especially compliance**: public speaking is important, but compliance people also need to understand the dynamics of selling and convincing others to support the compliance efforts. This builds on the sales techniques; see Chapter 10, "Selling Compliance (and the Importance of Your Job) to Management."

C. **Effective management of meetings to get results**: much corporate activity involves meetings bringing together different points of view. If meetings are not conducted carefully they can spin out of control and go in unexpected directions. Compliance leaders need to know how to get things done in meetings.

D. **Project management**: successful compliance programs require the ability to make things happen in a timely and cost effective manner, including major projects. For a multi-national company it can be an enormous task, for example, to draft and socialize a code of conduct that applies to all employees around the world. Training thousands of employees, conducting risk assessment sessions, and ensuring there is a company-wide functioning compliance infrastructure all require the coordination of activities and organizations throughout the company.

E. **Interpersonal skills/Active listening**: compliance people need to be able to listen carefully and attentively to others. This is especially true for investigators, auditors and ombudsmen, but it applies also for most compliance and ethics activities.

Appendix 9B

University of Pennsylvania Corporate Lawyering Seminar: Compliance Basics

A. What We Are Discussing: Organizational Control and Exposure—Corporate Liability
   1. Originally, Corporations Not Criminally Liable Until Early 20th Century
   2. Corporations Held Liable for Employee Acts within Scope of Employment
   3. Expansion to Negligence and No-Fault
   4. Increasing Scope and Penalties
   5. Using Criminal Law to Regulate

B. Compliance With What?
   1. Areas of Compliance Focus
      a. WWII Price Controls/Rationing
      b. Antitrust—*1960's*
      c. Foreign Bribery—*1970's*
      d. Insider Trading—*Late 1980's*
      e. Government Contract Fraud
      f. Banking/S&Ls
      g. Healthcare Fraud
      h. Earnings Management/Accounting Fraud
      i. Federal Law/State Law/Tort Law/Foreign Jurisdictions

C. What Are The Compliance And Ethical Risks The U of Pennsylvania Would Need To Consider In Its Compliance Program?—*Board These*
   1. Can A Large Organization Escape?
      a. Increasing Breadth of Risks and Restrictions
      b. A "City with/50,000 Population"—Avoiding any employee misconduct is not possible
      c. How the Government Finds Out—Examples of how cases come to light

D. The Trend: Good Citizen Corporation
   1. What Was Wrong With The Old Way?

       a. In Punishing Organizations It Is Impossible to Hit a Satisfactory Target

          i. Employees?

          ii. Stock Holders?

          iii. Creditors?

          iv. Senior Management?

          v. Guilty Individuals?

          vi. The Andersen example

       b. Litigation and Government Enforcement Only Kick In After the Damage Is Done

    2. The New Model

       a. Prevent

       b. Detect

       c. Report

       d. Correct

E. The Organizational Sentencing Guidelines

    1. What And Why Of The Guidelines

    2. Prevent And Detect Misconduct

    3. Made A Commitment

    4. Set A Standard

    5. The 2004 Revisions

    6. Blakely, Booker And Current Status

F. What Are The Elements Of A Compliance Program—The 7 Steps And More

    1. Review of Each of the Elements, As Applied in Best Practices Companies

G. Legal Developments After The Guidelines

    1. Other Agencies—EPA, HHS

    2. Caremark

    3. Ellerth And Kolstad

    4. Consent Decrees And Enforcement Authorities

       a. CSLG's experience In The Western District of Pennsylvania.

    5. Voluntary Disclosure And Immunity

    6. SOX and NYSE/NASDAQ

    7. International And Trends

       a. Australia—AS 3806

       b. Italy—Anti-bribery Legislation

    c. South Africa, JSE Standards

    d. Canada's Competition Bureau

    e. Privacy—EU, Canada

    f. EU/US On Competition Law

    g. India—Listing Standards

H. Class Exercise

    1. Class divided into 7 teams

    2. Each team recommends compliance steps in one Guidelines area for the University's compliance program to be able to present to a prosecutor to argue for mitigation

Appendix 9C

Certified Compliance & Ethics Professional (CCEP) Program Overview

Excerpted from the CCEP Candidate Handbook,
Society of Corporate Compliance and Ethics

Certification

The purpose of certification is to promote compliance and ethics through the certification of qualified compliance and ethics professionals by:

1. Recognizing formally those individuals who meet the eligibility requirements of the SCCE and pass the Certified Compliance & Ethics Professional (CCEP) Examination.

2. Encouraging continued personal and professional growth in the practice of compliance and ethics.

3. Providing a national standard of requisite knowledge required for certification; thereby assisting employers, the public and members of the professions in the assessment of a compliance and ethics professional.

Testing Agency

The SCCE has contracted with Applied Measurement Professionals, Inc. (AMP) to assist in the development, administration, scoring and analysis of its Certified Compliance & Ethics Professional (CCEP) Examination. AMP services also include the processing of examination applications and the reporting of scores to candidates who take the examination.

About the Examination

The examination is designed to test a well-defined body of knowledge representative of professional practice in the discipline. Successful completion of a certification examination verifies broad-based knowledge in the discipline being tested.

The examination leads to a certification credential in a compliance and ethics discipline defined by a role delineation study. The study involved surveying practitioners in the field to identify tasks that professionals routinely perform and consider important. Each edition of the certification examination is constructed in accordance with examination specifications that list content categories and tasks to be covered and assign numbers of test items and cognitive complexity to content categories. Specifications are developed to represent tasks that are performed in professional practice.

The CCEP examination is developed through a combined effort of qualified content experts and testing professionals. They review the test items to ensure that they are accurate in their content, relevant to practice and representative of good testing procedures.

This handbook provides specific information related to the Certified Compliance & Ethics Professional Examination. Individuals who meet eligibility requirements and who successfully pass this examination attain the Certified Compliance & Ethics Professional (CCEP) designation. To apply for this examination, complete the application included with this handbook and mail it to the address provided. This handbook can also be found on SCCE's Website (www.corporatecompliance.org).

Eligibility Requirements

To be eligible for the Certified Compliance & Ethics Professional (CCEP) Examination, candidates must fulfill the requirements in each of the following categories.

A. **Work Experience:** Candidates must meet **one** of the following criteria:
    Active Compliance Professional
    Have a minimum of one year of full-time work experience in compliance and ethics, with at least 50 percent of job duties dedicated to compliance and ethics, namely, those tasks reflected in the exam content outline.
    Allied Professional
    Have a minimum of 1,500 hours of work experience in compliance and ethics, performing tasks reflected in the exam content outline, obtained over a period not to exceed two years.
    Student
    Students who complete the compliance coursework from an SCCE accredited university program. Candidates must complete Section 2 on the SCCE Examination Application, indicating which one of the three criteria they meet.

B. **Continuing Education**
All candidates must submit twenty credits of continuing education received in the 12 month period preceding the date of the application. At least two credits must be documented in each content subject area (see list below).
*   Application of Management Practices for the Compliance Professional
*   Application of Personal and Business Ethics in Compliance
*   Written Compliance Policies and Procedures

- Designation of Compliance Officers and Committees
- Compliance Training and Education
- Communication and Reporting Mechanisms in Compliance
- Enforcement of Compliance Standards and Discipline
- Auditing and Monitoring for Compliance
- Response to Compliance Violations and Corrective Actions
- Complying with Government Regulations

CCEP credits are accumulated by participating in accredited seminars, workshops and conferences, completion of a self-test related to an accredited published article, use of accredited educational products, writing for publication, or serving as an instructor or facilitator of compliance-related education. A list of accredited activities is available through the SCCE administrative office or on the SCCE Website at www.corporatecompliance.org.

Only those programs accredited by SCCE or hosted by SCCE accredited providers will be recognized for credit. Providers of continuing education wishing to apply for accreditation may contact the SCCE administrative office to request the SCCE Accreditation Guidelines.

For questions regarding the CCEP certification program, contact:
Society of Corporate Compliance & Ethics
6500 Barrie Road, Suite 250
Minneapolis, MN 55435, United States
Phone +1 952 933 4977 or 888 277 4977 | Fax +1 952 988 0146
email: ccep@corporatecompliance.org
Web: www.corporatecompliance.org

Endnotes

1. See http://www.quinnipiac.edu/x16648.xml
2. See Paul E. McGreal, "Teaching Corporate Compliance: One Law School's Seminar Approach," *ethikos* 19, no. 1 (July/Aug 2005). Professor McGreal has since moved to Southern Illinois University in Carbondale, Illinois.
3. See http://www.theecoa.org/
4. See http://www.corporatecompliance.org/
5. See http://www.hcca-info.org
6. See http://www.compliance.org.au
7. See http://www.dii.org/
8. See http://www.ombudsassociation.org/
9. See http://www.complianceinstitute.co.uk
10. See http://www.int-comp.org
11. See http://www.pli.edu/
12. See http://www.conference-board.org/
13. See http://www.acca.com/
14. See http://www.abanet.org/
15. See http://www.americanconference.com

10   Selling Compliance (and the Importance of Your Job) to Management

Introduction

You are always selling in this field. It is a necessary skill. By this we do not mean anything cynical such as misleading companies into buying something they do not need. Rather, this means the ability to convince others of the need for a good compliance program and the need for their support. Selling is part of being in an organization; it goes with the territory.

When attempting to start a program, selling begins with management and the board. In the beginning, the compliance advocate has to convince management and the board of the need for a program, and the seriousness of the commitment. But even after the initial sale, you have to continue selling, to keep compliance a priority and get daily buy in. It is important not to think of this effort as a one-time project. You will need to earn the ongoing support of management and the board to bring the program up to an effective level, and then to keep it energized over the long term. You will also need to deal with employees in their everyday work. In your training and other communications you need to reach all those who work for the company so they understand the value of the program and the need to do the right thing, every day in every part of the business.

We offer here a number of tools—eight "sales tips"—to help in your task.[1] These sales tips have been organized for ease of reference, but you may want to mix and match those things that will work for you and your organization. To use these effectively, you need to know your audience. Certain points will appeal more to some audiences than to others. So pick and choose, but do not overwhelm or dilute key messages. In Appendix 10A, we have provided a quick list of some of the benefits of an effective program; this list is also useful if you are asked to do a cost-benefit analysis of the program.

The Sales Tips

1. *Avoiding the Big Legal Stick.*

The parade of horribles can be an effective tool for selling a compliance program to any organization. When most managers think of compliance, this is one of the things they probably picture first—all the bad things that can happen because of a violation. It is generally what initially gets people's attention, and the most common reason used for programs. You should recognize that fear has limits as a motivator; we do not recommend relying on fear as the sole reason for a program. However, there is no denying that, for many, it does get attention. In the legal world of today, there are many frightening things out there.

Avoiding violations—preventing trouble from happening—is a powerful motivator in organizations. For someone contemplating a compliance program, the most basic expectation would be that a program would prevent problems. This benefit is an important point to make, but be careful not to over promise. No organization with large numbers of people can expect to prevent everything. Consider, for example, that a company with tens of thousands of employees may be the size of an entire city. Who would expect a city to have all its residents avoid all offenses all the time? Similarly, while a company should strive for perfection, the compliance person must be careful never to promise this outcome. Still, even with that caveat, prevention is an important reason.

One starting point in raising compliance-consciousness is to discuss the increase in criminal risks. Any businessperson will know that there are more laws and rules with each passing year, and the legal environment grows ever more complex. Along with this trend is the fact of increasing criminal enforcement and the appearance of more enforcement officials. Civil and administrative violations, by themselves, can be serious with potentially astronomical costs. But the government is not content with this. Especially in the United States, we tend to use criminal law more as a regulatory tool. Each new scandal seems to push the enforcement line from the civil side to the criminal side.

Along with this shift toward criminalization is the reality that the accompanying penalties are severe and increasing: prison terms are becoming longer and fines seem to be taking on the role of a major revenue source for government. One example that illustrates this concept is the 2004 amendments to American antitrust law. Antitrust corporate fines had previously been capped at $10 million (although a separate law covering alternative minimum fines provided for much larger amounts.) Congress increased this ten-fold to $100 million. Individuals' fines were increased from $350,000 to $1 million. Prison terms increased from 3 to 10 years, to keep up with so many other increased prison terms for other offenses (it seems enforcers compete with one another to see who can get the most bang for the buck!). Predicting the future can be risky, but there is probably no risk in the prediction that there will be more rising penalties as time passes. In making this point to management it can be useful to present a "rogues gallery," illustrating these trends by listing some of the top fines and the companies hit with them.

2. Protect the Brand and Company Reputation.

The legal system is not the only source of damage to a company that is caught in improper conduct. Even if a company has not broken the law, if the public sees conduct it does not like, it can hammer a company through the marketplace. One need only recall the cases of prominent brands being attacked by consumer boycotts.

Bad news about a company can dramatically affect consumer appeal. The state of the environment, for example, is a popular cause among citizens. News that a company is polluting excessively, or has caused a major ecological disaster, can kill its image and cost a fortune in future revenue and PR-costs. Harassment and discrimination cases can alienate important customer groups. Word that the NAACP has contacted a company can be enough to raise a public outcry. Between television and the Internet, the entire customer base is capable of hearing any allegation within minutes; even a small-town exposé can break into market-affecting news. Of course, issues of product or service safety offer the clearest examples. One dangerous product can wipe out a company's market; the horror stories in this arena are legendary.

Furthermore, such bad news typically batters the stock. You can remind managers of the hit Martha Stewart's company's stock took when news of her legal troubles broke. Consider the value today of names like Enron, Andersen, and WorldCom. Suffice it is to say, they have no value, other than as warnings. The loss in market value in such cases is startling. And, of course, immediately behind such losses is the plaintiffs' bar.

3. It's Not Optional.

There may have been a day, not so long ago, when a company could just decide to take its chances with any compliance efforts, perhaps on the faith that all their employees were good folks who would never go astray. But it now appears that the government and others are not as inclined to depend on the good faith of companies and their employees. Increasingly, compliance efforts are moving from the voluntary category to the mandatory.[2] Consider, for example, Sarbanes-Oxley, which imposes (or pressures companies to adopt) certain compliance program elements. SOX, as it is unaffectionately known, applies to any publicly traded company in the U.S. Under this law, any company listed on a stock exchange must have a system for anonymous and confidential internal reporting of financial fraud. Every company affected by SOX must either have a code of conduct for its CEO and CFO, or explain why it does not. Lawyers who work for such companies on SEC matters have a compliance-reporting obligation. And the law provides protection for whistleblowers, including those who use internal reporting systems.

Following this cue, the New York Stock Exchange (NYSE) and the NAS-DAQ now require their listed companies to have codes of conduct and to post them on their Websites. Boards are now charged with greater diligence. But the mandate does not stop there. More companies are seeing the risk of dealing with suppliers and other business partners who may get them in trouble by their misconduct. Even companies, therefore, are starting to require compliance steps through their contracts with suppliers and other business partners. We are approaching the point where some customers will not do business with a company unless it has a compliance program, given that liability can extend to those who do business with law-breakers.

Finally, in those cases where a violation occurs, the government requires compliance programs as a condition of settlement. It is now quite common to find compliance program requirements in consent decrees, settlements and corporate integrity agreements. Of course, at that point the issue of how best to develop a compliance program becomes somewhat moot—the issue then shifts to how to meet the demands of the government.

The point for managers to understand is that there is just no sense in pretending that this need for compliance programs is something that does not apply to your company. With each new corporate scandal and each new legislative session, it becomes more likely that these things will be required. Given all the risks associated with not having a program, and all the other benefits available from an effective program, it makes no sense to wait to have one artificially forced on the company. Better to get the benefits and at the same time accept reality.

4. *It Can't Happen Here.*

In a company that has seen no problems itself, managers may think there is no reason to worry. Trouble may have hit other companies, but management will often dismiss those stories as something that only happens to other companies or other industries. The reality, however, can be quite different. For any company employing human beings, the odds are very high that there will be at least a few disturbing examples within the company. To bring this point home, consider doing a compliance audit to see what you can find. This can involve a limited number of interviews and employee file reviews. With any luck (or bad luck), you will find examples that can help convince management that they need to take a more pro-active approach to preventing misconduct. After all, if *you* can find it, investigative agencies or the government can find it.

Consider some of the examples of internal documents that have appeared before. In an infamous case involving Montgomery Ward, a Sears executive encouraged colleagues to recruit key Ward employees. The executive went so far as to send an email including the now-classic line, "Let's be predatory about it!" Eventually, that line was used in court against Sears. If you know where to look, it often does not take too much digging to find equally scary examples in your own backyard. Nothing is quite so convincing as an example from a company's own files.

5. *It's a Global Trend.*

One source of resistance, especially at multinational companies, is the opinion that this is just some peculiar American thing, part of a litigation obsession. Whether it is convincing a Paris headquarters or a Mexican field office, being able to show that this trend is global helps soften such resistance. To convince a multinational audience, it is important not to make your sales focus American. The discussion should not focus on the Sentencing Guidelines, but should reference its standards carefully in the discussion. It is best to emphasize that the seven steps in the Sentencing Guidelines are good, universal management steps. The average person will not understand why these steps would come from something related to sentencing (not every system is as punitive as the American one). Even in the U.S., the Guidelines standards are really not, in fact, as important at sentencing as they are at the prosecution point.

Depending on who your audience is in a global business, lead with some of the overseas compliance examples. For example, in the area of privacy protection, it is not the U.S. that has taken the lead in setting rules or establishing compliance standards. In this area companies around the world are struggling with how to meet European, not American, legal requirements. In addressing an audience in Europe, there is no need to lead with stories about Enron and WorldCom when they have their own tales of woe in Parmalat and Shell. In the area of antitrust enforcement, while the Americans hold the record for the largest antitrust fine ($500 million), E.U. enforcers are not far behind, and have the ability to impose fines equal to 10 percent of a company's world turnover. The American anti-bribery law, the FCPA, may have been the first, but an international treaty accepted by OECD members and other major trading nations has made this a global restriction. For example, in one recent case of alleged bribery in Kazakhstan, it was the Swiss bankers who broke news of suspicious activity. So if you are called upon to convince a headquarters in Amsterdam, or address sales people in Japan, do your research and come prepared to talk about examples in the countries where they do business, and not just the United States.

Once you have convinced your audience that the enforcement risks are universal, you can then explain to them that compliance programs are also part of the global scene. One of the most firmly established examples is in Australia. There the Australian Standards organization has promulgated a detailed standard on compliance programs, AS 3806. The Australasian Compliance Institute, a membership organization dedicated to the promotion of effective compliance programs, has as many members as the United States' ECOA, in a country with only 19 million people. These compliance initiatives are strongly supported by the government, particularly by the ACCC, the competition law and consumer protection enforcement arm. Other examples stand out in places like Canada, the E.U., and South Africa.

Ultimately, you can remind your audience of the underlying and compelling logic of why this development is inevitable and international. Society simply cannot allow large organizations to cause widespread and devastating harm. The fallout of corporate blunders can destroy lives and disrupt economies. Realistically, there will never be enough police to control organizations' misconduct before it happens. Some organizations have tens of thousands or hundreds of thousands of employees, often spread out all over the world. No one government is in position to control these organizations, even if one were inclined to commit the necessary resources. So there is no real choice than to pressure and induce organizations to police themselves.

6. Protect the Company from Waste, Fraud and Abuse.

One of the greatest potential benefits of a vigorous compliance program is the ability to protect the company from being a victim of waste, fraud and abuse. The very same techniques that help prevent your company from harming others will also help protect your company from being victimized. Such compliance fundamentals as helplines, investigations, auditing, internal control systems, monitoring, and risk profiling all can lead to prevention and detection of misconduct targeting the company.

What are the potential savings involved in this? The Association of Certified Fraud Examiners estimates companies lose the equivalent of 6 percent of their revenues to fraud.[3] This is an enormous toll, and considerably greater than the cost of even an extraordinarily ambitious compliance effort. Companies have also lost billions in unauthorized trading schemes, such as those that have made the headlines. This is one of the arguments you can make that can show a real financial return. You can develop this argument with the help of your company's risk management, loss management, security and insurance folks. They may be able to provide useful examples and support you if they think you are championing their cause.

Always keep in mind a point of caution, however, whenever you are arguing specific financial benefits from compliance programs. If the program is very effective you may actually suppress the worst abuses and ironically have smaller numbers to prove the program's benefit. You also do not want to appear to be suggesting that compliance and ethics efforts should only be undertaken if they produce specific financial results; this approach can come across as cynically mercenary. So when you use these types of specific savings as an argument, always include some of the other benefits as well.

7. *It's the Right Thing to Do.*

This might be surprising to some, but many people in business do believe in doing the right thing. It is a simple, straightforward point; there is not always an ulterior motive. This ethical motive has intrinsic appeal to many audiences. For example, in an informal survey of the sales tips conducted by one of the authors at a seminar on compliance that was predominantly for lawyers, "doing the right thing" was rated as the best reason. As you meet with employees and officers you will find that this approach offers a powerful force for many.

From a practical perspective, including this reason also helps keep the whole project less mercenary and thus more credible to internal and external audiences. Remember that the public expects companies to do the right thing, even if they are typically cynical concerning that motive.

8. *Taking the Offensive.*

Seizing the initiative can be one of the best and most appealing advantages of having a good program. The idea is that compliance is not just a cost, but an opportunity to add value to the business. This approach offers a more positive and exciting reason for endorsing a compliance program. It puts the compliance advocates in the position of sharing the quest for the company's success.

There can be a real marketing benefit today from having an effective program. Blue chip companies may look for this in prospective business partners. In one recent example a salesperson for a company happened to mention their newly enhanced program to a major corporate customer. The customer's people immediately wanted to know all about it. It turned out that the customer had a longstanding commitment to compliance and was excited to see a similar effort in a supplier. The sales person then reported back to headquarters on how helpful it was to be able to tell customers about the company's program.

Business customers may have this interest in your company's program because of the standards of the Sentencing Guidelines. The revised Guidelines speak of training "agents, as appropriate," on compliance matters. The supplier who is a step ahead and already provides relevant training to its employees who deal with that customer will have an advantage in the marketplace.

Having an effective program can also help in recruiting and retaining good people—both employees and board members. The existence of a compliance and ethics program is something that increasingly matters more to employees, having seen what happened to employees at Enron and Andersen. A compliance program protects and serves everyone, from the hourly employees to the senior officers and board members. No one wants to lose their retirement nest egg like the Enron employees, or have on their resume that they worked for a company now seen as a criminal enterprise. No one wants the embarrassment of being the target of friends' and neighbors' taunts and criticisms because of where they work.

There is also a benefit to companies when they educate employees on the legal environment. Employees who learn and understand the company's legal rights can help protect the company. This approach is not just about avoiding losses from compliance errors: the same educational effort used for preventive purposes can also serve a competitive purpose. Employees can learn that the law is not just a list of restrictions on the company; for smart companies it is also a tool to help compete more effectively.

There are, then, tangible commercial benefits for taking an aggressive approach to compliance. But, you need to be careful that you do not come across as too mercenary, or too calculating. You want management to support this effort for many reasons, not just the financial impact it offers. But it is always good to have a positive side to your presentation when trying to win people over to your way of thinking.

Other Sales Hints

There are of course more approaches to selling compliance, but remember that you must still be aware of your audience. Analyze what each group and each person wants. Some will see the program as a way for them to achieve an objective that is on their to-do lists. (Be careful, of course, not to undermine the compliance program in catering to potential supporters, and do not promise what you cannot deliver.) Some may have been at other companies when something went wrong, and want to avoid that miserable experience again. They may be able to support with real-world examples the danger elements mentioned in some of your points. Be careful, however, of any negative experiences these people may have had with a compliance program in their old company. Be able to explain how your program will be better and not make the same mistakes. Other people will just want compliance off their checklists, while some will have concerns about specific compliance issues, and see your program as a way to surface them.

You will need to think strategically about the people you are dealing with. You need to win their buy-in for the program. Try to bring others in at the program's formative stages. People are more likely to support something if they feel a degree of ownership. This helps avoid the we/they splits that arise in organizations. It is important to consider who the key players in the company are, and who can help you to get the program accepted. These people may hold key resources or be viewed as "thought leaders" in the company. Consider what will appeal most to them. Discuss compliance with others and see who shares your interest. Delegate to those who are interested and capable. This tactic not only helps get the work done, but can be critical for building support and understanding.

In order to achieve success and avoid the pitfalls, you need to recognize the ins and outs of group and organizational dynamics. Know your culture and what is acceptable. Some companies are touchy-feely; some are very business-like. Some are decentralized; some are command and control operations. Play to their preferences. Know which companies your company admires–find out about those companies' compliance programs. Use the sorts of aids most likely to grab attention, including the use of well-known speakers, dramatic videos, or detailed packets of information (including the results of your preliminary audit—see Sales Tip 4, above). You can get help on this effort from companies that produce videos and other materials dealing with all aspects of compliance.

Meetings are a common tool in companies for getting things done, but beware of the risks: meetings can be unpredictable. Just as in a debate, a lot of unexpected objections and information can be thrown your way. Prepare your facts and arguments well in advance and practice your presentations. (Any compliance person should be trained in effective public speaking.) It is especially important to avoid surprising people at meetings. Discomfort is a seller's worst enemy. Meetings may take on the tone of whoever speaks first, be they cautious, excited or just adamantly opposed to everything you are suggesting. One or two strong voices can turn an entire meeting into a fiasco. To control this risk, always check with the participants in advance so you know what to expect. Speak to the thought leaders and any potential detractors beforehand so you can address their concerns specifically.

You may also find it effective to take advantage of outside speakers. Sometimes having someone from outside say these things can be more powerful than if they come from a familiar insider. A consultant, or someone from a peer company, may have more impact than you, even when they say exactly the same things. Of course, be careful not to enlist anyone who is looking for a job, lest you find yourself usurped.

The close

You have followed our tips and met with some success. Now you are faced with negotiating what the arrangement will be. When you get to the topic of your own authority and goals for the company's compliance program, should you "settle"? What if management agrees to do a little, but not much? Is it better to at least have something rather than nothing?

This can be a truly difficult question. In the corporate world, going along and compromising is generally a value; in compliance, accepting compromises that gut the program can destroy all your efforts. It can make you, personally and professionally, look bad. If future confrontations affecting the program occur, your position may be too weak for you to act effectively. If violations occur, this weakness can be especially risky, even leading to your potential complicity in misconduct. Of course each circumstance about the program requires individual consideration. But if you give up key points at the start, there is a high risk you will never get those things in the program, until the company gets into trouble because the program lacked what it needed. And then you may be the one held responsible for establishing a weak program!

But if you appear to be just stubborn or ungrateful, it can easily hurt your career. This example demonstrates why you have to be tough, but politically adept, if you want to go into this field. If you agree to a limited program, make it clear on the record what you think should be in the program. But be careful you do not create a document that can kill the company in litigation.

Your last challenge will be closing the sale. Be sure to "ask for the order." Your proposal for a compliance program needs to be specific, leaving no doubts where possible. In the key decision-making meeting, have a specific plan ready to go, so there is something they can say "yes" to. At the very least, have the infrastructure plan set out. Realistically, management will want some idea of the spending required. It may help to have charts and other media for more detailed explanations of your plans. You should set a timetable for implementation and finally, of course, put yourself in the picture at this point.

Once you have management's agreement, get going immediately. Get the foundations in place ASAP. Request a board resolution, so there is no backing up or backing out. Get it in writing. Such a document will be important as proof of board support if the integrity of the program is ever challenged. To aid in implementation, make sure everyone affected in the company is notified, and make sure you, or whoever is meant to run the program, have the authority to do what needs to be done. You are now on your way!

Appendix 10A

Benefits of a Compliance Program

1. Avoid/reduce criminal fines
2. Avoid/reduce criminal charges
3. Avoid/reduce punitive damages
4. Avoid civil liability
5. Avoid imposition of adversaries' counsel fees, e.g., in antitrust cases
6. Avoid government suspension/debarment
7. Avoid loss of export privileges
8. Help in recruiting/retaining employees
9. Maintain high employee morale/productivity
10. Avoid loss of personnel from charges/convictions/dismissals
11. Help in recruiting/retaining board members
12. Prevent/reduce waste, fraud and abuse against company by employees and contractors
13. Competitive advantage in selling to blue chip customers
14. Protect/strengthen brand reputation
15. Avoid consumer boycotts
16. Avoid/reduce consumer informal complaints (phone calls, letters, emails)
17. Maintain goodwill with governments, i.e., regulators & legislators
18. Reduce insurance costs
19. Avoid/reduce litigation against board members
20. Avoid/reduce outside legal counsel fees from compliance litigation
21. Avoid/reduce management disruption from litigation, investigations, or compliance crises
22. Avoid costs of imposed compliance programs, such as monitors and third-party reviews
23. Avoid limits on future business freedom from government-imposed restrictions
24. Avoid loss of stock market value
25. Avoid/reduce loss of company's own proprietary information (through IP compliance program)
26. Strengthen protection of company's own intellectual property, i.e., trademarks, copyrighted materials, and patents
27. Reduce generation and retention of excess records (through records compliance program)
28. Avoid/reduce loss of life and property, and down time from unsafe facilities/activities and accidents

Endnotes

1. In our larger text, (Joseph E. Murphy and Joshua H. Leet, *Working for Integrity: Finding the Perfect Job in the Rapidly Growing Compliance and Ethics Field* (Minneapolis: Society of Corporate Compliance and Ethics, 2006)), we provide additional tips and greater detail.

2. See Joseph E. Murphy, "'Mandavolent' Compliance," *ethikos* 19, no. 2 (Sept/Oct 2005).

3. Jonny Frank and Nancy Newman-Limata, "A New Audience for COSO–SEC & PCAOB Requirements for Anti-Fraud Programs & Control," *Prevention of Corporate Liability Current Report* 12, no. 3, (BNA, April 19, 2004).

Appendices

Appendix A

Glossary and Acronyms in Compliance

Excerpted from *Compliance Primer: A Guide to the World of Corporate Ethics and Compliance Programs*, by Joseph Murphy

Published by Integrity Interactive | http://www.integrity-interactive.com

Glossary of Compliance Terms

Agents   Those who do business on behalf of a company but who are independent from the company and are not employees, are considered agents. Whether a company is legally liable for what its agents do is a difficult legal question that can vary case by case. The Sentencing Guidelines requirements for training and communications and for having a system for obtaining advice and reporting concerns apply to a company's agents.

Antitrust Division   The unit in the U.S. Department of Justice responsible for enforcing federal antitrust (e.g., price fixing) laws.

Audit committee   The committee of a corporation's board of directors responsible for overseeing financial controls. In companies listed on any US national securities exchange, all members of this committee must be "independent," i.e., not managers of the company. Some companies use this committee to oversee their compliance programs.

Auditing   Auditing may be used as a technical term, referring to certain reviews conducted according to auditing standards. In the compliance context, the term usually means reviews of systems, standards, activities, etc., of the company, conducted after the fact. These reviews usually involve sampling. The Sentencing Guidelines require auditing as one of the steps for assuring that a compliance program is effective. (See "monitoring," covering real time reviews).

Background check   Companies conduct checks on the backgrounds of potential employees (or, sometimes, employees being promoted) to determine whether they have engaged in misconduct, have a prior conviction, have a suspended drivers license, etc. The Sentencing Guidelines include a requirement that companies be careful in whom they give responsibility to. There is also potential civil liability for companies for negligence in hiring employees who subsequently cause harm.

Best practices   Companies wanting to assure that their compliance programs are state of the art seek to determine what are the best approaches being used by others. These approaches are referred to as best practices.

Caremark   The *Caremark* case is an opinion by the Chancery Court in Delaware, warning corporate directors that they should consider having compliance programs. Otherwise, they might face personal liability for misconduct that a compliance program might have prevented or detected. This court is highly influential on matters of corporate law.

CBT or computer-based training   Training can be provided to employees using computers, either by CD-ROM or over the Web. Web-based training may be through a company's Intranet, or over the Internet. Advantages of Web-based training include the ability to reach employees everywhere at a low cost, to record automatically the employees' completion of the training, and to test employees' understanding of the subject. Integrity Interactive specializes in interactive on-line training that engages employees.

Chief compliance officer   In larger, more complex organizations there may be multiple compliance officers. The highest-ranking compliance officer, typically at the organization's headquarters, may be designated the chief compliance officer.

Code of conduct   Companies adopt codes of conduct to set their standards of conduct on compliance and ethical issues. These manuals go by many names, including codes of ethics and business practice guides. They help meet item 1 of the Sentencing Guidelines compliance standards. Codes are required for all companies listed on the NYSE and NASDAQ. In addition, under Sarbanes-Oxley, all publicly traded companies must either have a code of ethics for their top financial officers and CEO or explain why not.

Compliance committee   Compliance committees are part of a company's compliance infrastructure. Committees are typically composed of managers who participate in company-wide compliance and ethics efforts.

Compliance officer   Also known as "ethics officer" or similar terms, a compliance officer is the senior manager responsible for managing the company compliance program. This position helps meet item two of the Sentencing Guidelines compliance standards.

Compliance program A compliance program is a system of management steps to prevent and detect misconduct. The most commonly used standard for these programs in the U.S. is the Sentencing Guidelines.

Consent decree Litigation is sometimes settled by entering into an agreement that is signed by the judge and entered as a court order. Violations of these orders, or consent decrees, are punishable as contempt of court. These orders may contain provisions requiring institution of a compliance program.

Corporate Integrity Agreement When health care providers settle allegations of Medicare/Medicaid fraud the government typically requires implementation of a compliance program under a corporate integrity agreement ("CIA").

Deep dive In order to assess and measure compliance, companies may use this management concept that involves an intensive review of particular business units and operations. This has the intensity of an audit with a broader scope. See Murphy, "The Measurement Challenge: Introducing the Deep Dive," 17 *ethikos* 7 (May/Jun 2004).

DII The DII or Defense Industry Initiative is an organization of defense contractors formed in the 1980s in response to compliance issues in the defense industry. This group holds a best practices forum to compare members' compliance activities.

Disciplinary system The Sentencing Guidelines standards include having a system to ensure that discipline for violations of a company's standards are consistent and adequate. There must also be discipline for failure to take reasonable steps to prevent or detect criminal conduct.

DOJ DOJ or the Department of Justice, is the cabinet level agency of the U.S. government responsible for enforcing federal law, including federal criminal law. The department is organized by divisions, including the Antitrust Division (includes price-fixing enforcement) and the Criminal Fraud Division (includes FCPA enforcement).

Due diligence Due diligence is a legal term used in the Sentencing Guidelines. It represents the amount of effort required to meet the legal requirements. Meeting due diligence standards is not a rote or punch-list exercise; it requires an amount of effort based on the risk involved.

Ellerth   In the *Ellerth* case the U.S. Supreme Court ruled that a company's efforts to prevent harassment and its response to allegations of harassment may, in certain cases, serve as a legal defense to a harassment suit.

Enron   In 2001-2002, alleged accounting fraud and other scandals led to the bankruptcy of this once high-flying energy company. This was followed by a series of major corporate scandals involving such companies as Arthur Andersen, WorldCom, Tyco and HealthSouth that some have described with terms such as the Enron era cases.

ECOA or Ethics & Compliance Officer Association   ECOA, formerly Ethics Officer Association, is a non-profit organization consisting of those working in companies and other organizations with responsibility for compliance and ethics programs. You do not need to be an officer or an ethicist to join.

Ethics program   Companies sometimes refer to "ethics programs" instead of compliance programs, and some companies have both ethics and compliance efforts. "Ethics" programs are generally values oriented, and focus on doing the right or moral thing, not just what is legal. There is much debate about the role of "ethics" and "law" in programs, although it is likely that both require similar management techniques to be effective.

HCCA or Health Care Compliance Association   HCCA is a national organization of compliance practitioners in the health care industry.

Helpline or hotline   Companies provide employees with means to raise questions and report violations outside of the normal management chain of command. These typically involve toll-free phone lines that may be called hotlines, helplines, guidelines or similar terms. The term "hotline" has been criticized as having too much of a big brother overtone. The existence of such reporting systems helps meet item five of the Sentencing Guidelines compliance standards and can also be used to meet the reporting requirements of section 301 of Sarbanes-Oxley.

Holder memo   In 1999, an official in the Department of Justice, Eric Holder, issued a memo to the U.S. Attorneys offices addressing when to prosecute companies. The memo states that they should give credit to companies for having compliance programs, but also emphasizes the need for companies to voluntarily disclose violations. The memo favors companies waiving their privilege protections, which has been a very controversial issue. The Holder memo was subsequently updated by the Thompson memo in 2003.

Indictment   Prosecutors use indictments to charge individuals and companies with serious crimes. They do this by convening grand juries, which then determine whether there is sufficient reason to indict someone.

Industry practice   The Sentencing Guidelines standards include reference to a company's compliance program being at least as good as industry practice. This point in the guidelines makes it important that companies have some sense of what their peers are doing, to be sure they are at least as diligent.

Industry practice forums   Because of the Sentencing Guidelines' reference to industry practice, companies in some industries have formed industry practices forums to exchange information about compliance program approaches in their industry. The first of these were the best practices forums among members of the Defense Industry Initiative. Similar groups have also been formed on a geographic basis.

Investigation   When a company becomes aware of the possibility of a violation, it will typically take steps to determine the facts. Such investigations may be conducted by the company's own staff, or by an outside firm such as a law firm, accounting firm or an investigation firm.

Kolstad   In the *Kolstad* case, the U.S. Supreme Court ruled that in employment discrimination cases, what a company does to prevent discrimination, and how it responds to allegations, must be taken into consideration in deciding whether the company is subject to punitive damages. The message is that a compliance program may act as a defense to punitive damages.

Measurement   The Guidelines call on companies to evaluate periodically how effective their programs are. To conduct this type of measurement, companies use tools such as surveys, focus groups, audits and other types of reviews.

Monitoring   The Sentencing Guidelines say that an effective compliance program should include steps to ensure that the program is followed, including monitoring to detect criminal conduct. Monitoring is, in effect, the real time checking of performance. This contrasts with auditing, which is generally viewed as occurring after the fact, on a sampling basis. One example of monitoring would be the systems used to check on emissions of air pollutants.

Online or Web-based training   Employees can be trained through the use of the Internet in ways that were previously unavailable through live training. The training can be interactive and available 24 hours a day. Although use of video is generally not practical on the Internet, text, graphics and audio can be combined, along with an interesting story line, to make online training engaging and memorable for employees. Integrity Interactive uses this type of approach for employee training.

Privilege protection   Certain communications can be exempt from discovery or production in litigation. The most well known are communications with an attorney to seek confidential legal advice. There are, however, a number of other types of communications that may be subject to some protection under privilege. Managers should consult with their lawyers on how to assert and protect these privileges. They should also remember that even privileged communications should be written in a responsible manner and they should not assume that others will not see what they write.

Punitive damages   In private lawsuits the person suing may be able to recover punitive damages if the defendant's conduct is sufficiently bad. These damages can be enormous and are in addition to any criminal fines the government may pursue. It may be possible to use a company's compliance program as an argument against hitting it with punitive damages.

Qualified Legal Compliance Committee   Under rules promulgated by the SEC under Sarbanes Oxley, publicly traded companies may establish a committee of independent board of directors' members that establishes written procedures for handling reports of evidence of material violations brought forward by securities lawyers.

Retaliation or retribution   Retaliation or retribution refers to efforts to punish someone for raising ethical or compliance questions or reporting misconduct. Under the guidelines, systems to allow employees to report violations should come with an assurance of protection against retaliation. In addition, in certain areas of the law it is illegal to retaliate against whistleblowers.

Risk assessment or inventory   In order to design and implement an effective compliance program it is important to determine what the legal and ethical risks are. This calls for examination or assessment of those risks on a periodic basis. Such an assessment should include all of the business units in a company. Even a small subsidiary or division can cause enormous harm to a company through misconduct.

SCCE or The Society of Corporate Compliance and Ethics   SCCE is an international, non-profit membership organization solely dedicated to improving the quality of corporate governance, compliance and ethics. Anyone with an interest in compliance and ethics can join.

Self-assessment   One method of compliance review is the self-assessment, an approach first popular in the environmental area. In a typical self-assessment, the compliance office provides line managers with a set of standards, and requests the managers to assess their own organization's performance against those standards. These self-assessments may then be subject to audit.

Sentencing Commission   The Sentencing Commission or U.S. Sentencing Commission, is an agency of the federal judiciary that sets standards federal judges use when sentencing those convicted of federal crimes. In 1991 this commission issued standards that applied to sentencing of organizations, including corporations; these were revised in 2004. Previously the commission had issued standards for the sentencing of individuals.

Sentencing Guidelines   The Sentencing Guidelines, or Federal Sentencing Guidelines, are a set of standards for federal judges imposing sentences on those convicted of federal crimes. The Organizational Sentencing Guidelines apply to companies and other organizations. Among other things, these guidelines define what must be in a company's compliance program if that company is to be eligible for a reduced sentence if convicted. The standards require due diligence and seven specific items (e.g., standards and procedures, a disciplinary and incentive system, etc.). When people refer to the "seven standards" or the "guidelines," this is the standard they mean.

Standards and procedures   Item one of the guidelines' compliance standards requires companies to have standards and procedures designed to prevent and detect criminal conduct. Typically the starting point for companies is to adopt a code of conduct, but they also need to have internal controls.

Suspension and debarment   Those who do business with the government are subject to being excluded from doing any further business with the government (suspension or debarment), if they engage in certain offenses. A contractor can be suspended even before the government proves an actual violation.

Thompson memo   U.S. Deputy Attorney General Larry Thompson in 2003 updated the Holder memo by issuing a new memo to the U.S. Attorneys offices. Like the Holder memo, it addresses when to prosecute companies. The memo states that they should give credit to companies for having compliance programs, but also emphasizes the need for companies to voluntarily disclose violations. Unlike the Holder memo, this letter places much emphasis on the board of directors' role. The memo also favors companies waiving their privilege protections, which has been a very controversial issue.

U.S. Attorney   The United States is divided into fewer than 100 federal districts, each with a U.S. Attorney who is responsible for bringing federal cases in that district. These are the federal government's prosecutors; they are appointed by the president.

Voluntary disclosure   When a company discovers that its employees have engaged in criminal misconduct, the government wants those companies to voluntarily report the violation to the appropriate government agency. The Antitrust Division has a special program that gives the first company in an industry to report a criminal antitrust violation complete immunity from prosecution, as long as certain conditions are met. Most other agencies do not make such a commitment, but state that they will consider the fact that a company has voluntarily come forward.

WebLine^SM service   As an alternative to telephone helplines, companies can use a Web-based system to receive questions and concerns about compliance issues. The Integrity WebLine service is integrated into online training courses, so employees can raise questions during the training and at any other time issues arise. This system also provides anonymity.

Whistleblowers   Those in an organization who come forward and report wrongdoing are referred to as "whistleblowers." Under the Sentencing Guidelines standards, companies are expected to protect whistleblowers from retaliation. Under a federal statute, whistleblowers in companies that do business with the government may bring lawsuits on their own for the benefit of the government (called "qui tam" suits). They receive a percentage of the government's recovery, which can be an enormous amount of money.

Acronyms in Compliance

ACC...........Association of Corporate Counsel

ACI...........Australasian Compliance Institute

ACPA ....Association for Compliance Professionals of Australia (now ACI)

ADA ....Americans with Disabilities Act

AUSA ....Assistant U.S. Attorney

BNA...........Bureau of National Affairs

CBT...........Computer-based training

CCO ....Chief Compliance Officer

CCQ ....Corporate Conduct Quarterly

CIA ....Corporate Integrity Agreement

CO ....Compliance Officer

COSO........Council of Sponsoring Organizations

DII............Defense Industry Initiative

DOJ ....Department of Justice

ECOA ....Equal Credit Opportunity Act

ECOA ....Ethics & Compliance Officer Association

EEOC ....Equal Employment Opportunity Commission

EPA............Environmental Protection Agency

ERC..........Ethics Resource Center

ERISA ......Employee Retirement Income Security Act

EU.............European Union

FCPA ....Foreign Corrupt Practices Act

FCRA ....Fair Credit Reporting Act

FLSA ....Fair Labor Standards Act

FMLA........Family Medical Leave Act

FSG...........Federal Sentencing Guidelines

FTC ....Federal Trade Commission

HCCA ......Health Care Compliance Association

HHS ....Department of Health and Human Services

I-9.............Immigration form required for new employees

IIC ....Integrity Interactive Corporation

NLRA ....National Labor Relations Act

NLRB ....National Labor Relations Board

NYSE.........New York Stock Exchange

OIG ....Office of Inspector General

OSHA ....Occupational Safety and Health Administration

PAC ....Political Action Committee

QLCC ....Qualified Legal Compliance Committee

RCRA ....Resource Conservation and Recovery Act

SCCE........Society of Corporate Compliance and Ethics

SEC...........Securities and Exchange Commission

SME..........Subject Matter Expert

SOX ....Sarbanes-Oxley Act

USSC ....United States Sentencing Commission

VPPPA .....Voluntary Protection Program Participants Association

Appendix B

Sentencing Guidelines Definition

EFFECTIVE COMPLIANCE AND ETHICS PROGRAM §8B2.1.

Effective Compliance and Ethics Program

a. To have an effective compliance and ethics program, for purposes of subsection (f) of §8C2.5 (Culpability Score) and subsection (c)(1) of §8D1.4 (Recommended Conditions of Probation - Organizations), an organization shall—

   1. exercise due diligence to prevent and detect criminal conduct; and

   2. otherwise promote an organizational culture that encourages ethical conduct and a commitment to compliance with the law.

      Such compliance and ethics program shall be reasonably designed, implemented, and enforced so that the program is generally effective in preventing and detecting criminal conduct. The failure to prevent or detect the instant offense does not necessarily mean that the program is not generally effective in preventing and detecting criminal conduct.

b. Due diligence and the promotion of an organizational culture that encourages ethical conduct and a commitment to compliance with the law within the meaning of subsection (a) minimally require the following:

   1. The organization shall establish standards and procedures to prevent and detect criminal conduct.

   2. (A) The organization's governing authority shall be knowledgeable about the content and operation of the compliance and ethics program and shall exercise reasonable oversight with respect to the implementation and effectiveness of the compliance and ethics program.

      (B) High-level personnel of the organization shall ensure that the organization has an effective compliance and ethics program, as described in this guideline. Specific individual(s) within high-level personnel shall be assigned overall responsibility for the compliance and ethics program.

      (C) Specific individual(s) within the organization shall be delegated day-to-day operational responsibility for the compliance and ethics program. Individual(s) with operational responsibility shall report periodically to high-level personnel and, as appropriate, to the governing authority, or an appropriate subgroup of the governing authority, on the effectiveness of the compliance and ethics program. To carry out such operational responsibility, such individual(s) shall be given adequate resources, appropriate authority, and direct access to the governing authority or an appropriate subgroup of the governing authority.

3. The organization shall use reasonable efforts not to include within the substantial authority personnel of the organization any individual whom the organization knew, or should have known through the exercise of due diligence, has engaged in illegal activities or other conduct inconsistent with an effective compliance and ethics program.

4. (A) The organization shall take reasonable steps to communicate periodically and in a practical manner its standards and procedures, and other aspects of the compliance and ethics program, to the individuals referred to in subdivision (B) by conducting effective training programs and otherwise disseminating information appropriate to such individuals' respective roles and responsibilities.

   (B) The individuals referred to in subdivision (A) are the members of the governing authority, high-level personnel, substantial authority personnel, the organization's employees, and, as appropriate, the organization's agents.

5. The organization shall take reasonable steps—

   (A) to ensure that the organization's compliance and ethics program is followed, including monitoring and auditing to detect criminal conduct;

   (B) to evaluate periodically the effectiveness of the organization's compliance and ethics program; and

   (C) to have and publicize a system, which may include mechanisms that allow for anonymity or confidentiality, whereby the organization's employees and agents may report or seek guidance regarding potential or actual criminal conduct without fear of retaliation.

6. The organization's compliance and ethics program shall be promoted and enforced consistently throughout the organization through (A) appropriate incentives to perform in accordance with the compliance and ethics program; and (B) appropriate disciplinary measures for engaging in criminal conduct and for failing to take reasonable steps to prevent or detect criminal conduct.

7. After criminal conduct has been detected, the organization shall take reasonable steps to respond appropriately to the criminal conduct and to prevent further similar criminal conduct, including making any necessary modifications to the organization's compliance and ethics program.

c. In implementing subsection (b), the organization shall periodically assess the risk of criminal conduct and shall take appropriate steps to design, implement, or modify each requirement set forth in subsection (b) to reduce the risk of criminal conduct identified through this process.

Commentary

Application Notes:

1. *Definitions.—For purposes of this guideline:*

   'Compliance and ethics program' means a program designed to prevent and detect criminal conduct.

   'Governing authority' means the (A) the Board of Directors; or (B) if the organization does not have a Board of Directors, the highest-level governing body of the organization.

   'High-level personnel of the organization' and 'substantial authority personnel' have the meaning given those terms in the Commentary to §8A1.2 (Application Instructions - Organizations).

   'Standards and procedures' means standards of conduct and internal controls that are reasonably capable of reducing the likelihood of criminal conduct.

2. *Factors to Consider in Meeting Requirements of this Guideline.—*

   A. *In General.—Each of the requirements set forth in this guideline shall be met by an organization; however, in determining what specific actions are necessary to meet those requirements, factors that shall be considered include: (i) applicable industry practice or the standards called for by any applicable governmental regulation; (ii) the size of the organization; and (iii) similar misconduct.*

   B. *Applicable Governmental Regulation and Industry Practice.—An organization's failure to incorporate and follow applicable industry practice or the standards called for by any applicable governmental regulation weighs against a finding of an effective compliance and ethics program.*

   C. *The Size of the Organization.—*

      i. *In General.—The formality and scope of actions that an organization shall take to meet the requirements of this guideline, including the necessary features of the organization's standards and procedures, depend on the size of the organization.*

      ii. *Large Organizations.—A large organization generally shall devote more formal operations and greater resources in meeting the requirements of this guideline than shall a small organization. As appropriate, a large organization should encourage small organizations (espe-*

cially those that have, or seek to have, a business relationship with the large organization) to implement effective compliance and ethics programs.

iii. *Small Organizations.—In meeting the requirements of this guideline, small organizations shall demonstrate the same degree of commitment to ethical conduct and compliance with the law as large organizations. However, a small organization may meet the requirements of this guideline with less formality and fewer resources than would be expected of large organizations. In appropriate circumstances, reliance on existing resources and simple systems can demonstrate a degree of commitment that, for a large organization, would only be demonstrated through more formally planned and implemented systems.*

Examples of the informality and use of fewer resources with which a small organization may meet the requirements of this guideline include the following: (I) the governing authority's discharge of its responsibility for oversight of the compliance and ethics program by directly managing the organization's compliance and ethics efforts; (II) training employees through informal staff meetings, and monitoring through regular 'walk-arounds' or continuous observation while managing the organization; (III) using available personnel, rather than employing separate staff, to carry out the compliance and ethics program; and (IV) modeling its own compliance and ethics program on existing, well-regarded compliance and ethics programs and best practices of other similar organizations.

D. *Recurrence of Similar Misconduct.—Recurrence of similar misconduct creates doubt regarding whether the organization took reasonable steps to meet the requirements of this guideline. For purposes of this subdivision, 'similar misconduct' has the meaning given that term in the Commentary to §8A1.2 (Application Instructions - Organizations).*

3. *Application of Subsection (b)(2).—High-level personnel and substantial authority personnel of the organization shall be knowledgeable about the content and operation of the compliance and ethics program, shall perform their assigned duties consistent with the exercise of due diligence, and shall promote an organizational culture that encourages ethical conduct and a commitment to compliance with the law.*

If the specific individual(s) assigned overall responsibility for the compliance and ethics program does not have day-to-day operational responsibility for the program, then the individual(s) with day-to-day operational respon-

sibility for the program typically should, no less than annually, give the governing authority or an appropriate subgroup thereof information on the implementation and effectiveness of the compliance and ethics program.

4. *Application of Subsection (b)(3).—*

    A. *Consistency with Other Law.—Nothing in subsection (b)(3) is intended to require conduct inconsistent with any Federal, State, or local law, including any law governing employment or hiring practices.*

    B. *Implementation.—In implementing subsection (b)(3), the organization shall hire and promote individuals so as to ensure that all individuals within the high-level personnel and substantial authority personnel of the organization will perform their assigned duties in a manner consistent with the exercise of due diligence and the promotion of an organizational culture that encourages ethical conduct and a commitment to compliance with the law under subsection (a). With respect to the hiring or promotion of such individuals, an organization shall consider the relatedness of the individual's illegal activities and other misconduct (i.e., other conduct inconsistent with an effective compliance and ethics program) to the specific responsibilities the individual is anticipated to be assigned and other factors such as: (i) the recency of the individual's illegal activities and other misconduct; and (ii) whether the individual has engaged in other such illegal activities and other such misconduct.*

5. *Application of Subsection (b)(6).—Adequate discipline of individuals responsible for an offense is a necessary component of enforcement; however, the form of discipline that will be appropriate will be case specific.*

6. *Application of Subsection (c).—To meet the requirements of subsection (c), an organization shall:*

    A. *Assess periodically the risk that criminal conduct will occur, including assessing the following:*

       i. *The nature and seriousness of such criminal conduct.*

      ii. *The likelihood that certain criminal conduct may occur because of the nature of the organization's business. If, because of the nature of an organization's business, there is a substantial risk that certain types of criminal conduct may occur, the organization shall take reasonable steps to prevent and detect that type of criminal conduct. For example, an organization that, due to the nature of its business, employs sales personnel who have flexibility to set prices shall establish standards and procedures designed to prevent and detect price-fixing. An organization that, due to the nature of its business, employs sales personnel* who have flexibility to represent the material characteristics of a product shall establish standards and procedures designed to prevent and detect fraud.

    iii. The prior history of the organization. The prior history of an organization may indicate types of criminal conduct that it shall take actions to prevent and detect.

B. Prioritize periodically, as appropriate, the actions taken pursuant to any requirement set forth in subsection (b), in order to focus on preventing and detecting the criminal conduct identified under subdivision (A) of this note as most likely to occur.

C. Modify, as appropriate, the actions taken pursuant to any requirement set forth in subsection (b) to reduce the risk of criminal conduct identified under subdivision (A) of this note as most likely to occur.

Background: This section sets forth the requirements for an effective compliance and ethics program. This section responds to section 805(a)(2)(5) of the Sarbanes-Oxley Act of 2002, Public Law 107–204, which directed the Commission to review and amend, as appropriate, the guidelines and related policy statements to ensure that the guidelines that apply to organizations in this chapter 'are sufficient to deter and punish organizational criminal misconduct.'

The requirements set forth in this guideline are intended to achieve reasonable prevention and detection of criminal conduct for which the organization would be vicariously liable. The prior diligence of an organization in seeking to prevent and detect criminal conduct has a direct bearing on the appropriate penalties and probation terms for the organization if it is convicted and sentenced for a criminal offense.

Appendix C

Where Can I Get More Information and Advice?
Resources on employment in the compliance/ethics field

Articles:

Buss, Dale, "The Ethics Field Is Growing, But It's Tough to Break Into," *CareerJournal.com*, February 5, 2004.

Costa, Len, "The Rise of Compliance Man: Ignore Him at Your Peril," *Slate.com*, May 26, 2004.

Doyle, Anne, "You're Hired! Proposed Interview Questions to Ask a Prospective Compliance Professional," *Compliance Today* 7, no. 1 (2005).

Lauricella, Tom, "New Cops Will Walk the Mutual-Funds Beat," *Wall Street Journal*, April 16, 2004.

Mendels, Pamela, "The Rise of the Chief Privacy Officer: CPOs Are a New Breed of Execs That Combine Tech and Legal Savvy — and the Ability to Say No," *BusinessWeek Online*, December 14, 2000.

Murphy, Joseph, "Compliance Officers: One Part Ombudsman, Two Parts Watchdog," *National Law Journal* 15, no. 18 (1992).

Murphy, Joseph, "Enhancing the Compliance Officer's Authority: Preparing An Employment Contract," *ethikos* 11, no. 6 (May/June 1998).

Sammer, Joanne, "Chief Compliance Officers Define New Position, Responsibilities," *Compliance Week*, March 16, 2004.

Studies/Surveys:

Health Care Compliance Association, "8th Annual Survey, 2006 Profile of Health Care Compliance Officers." Very useful source of information about compliance work in the health care field, including salary data.

IAPP and the Ponemon Institute, "2005 Privacy Professional's Role, Function & Salary Survey." August 2005.

Books:

Adams, A., "So You Want To Work in the Health Care Compliance Field: Practical Advice on Developing a Career in Health Care Compliance," in Jan Christian Heller, Joseph E. Murphy and Mark E. Meaney, *Guide To Professional Development in Compliance* (Boston: Jones and Bartlett Publishers, 2001).

Murphy, Joseph E. and Joshua H Leet, *Working for Integrity: Finding the Perfect Job in the Rapidly Growing Compliance and Ethics Field* (Minneapolis: Society of Corporate Compliance and Ethics, 2006).

Compliance and ethics organizations:

The Auditing Roundtable, 15111 N. Hayden Road, Suite #160355, Scottsdale, Arizona 85260-2555, phone 480-659-3738, email kathy@auditing-roundtable.org, Website http://www.auditing-roundtable.org/. A professional organization dedicated to the development and professional practice of environmental, health and safety auditing. Provides a link to assist in connecting employers with potential employees.

Australasian Compliance Institute is open to anyone interested in the field of compliance/ethics. It provides email notices to members about new job openings in the compliance field in Australia. The Web address is: http://compliance.org.au/www_aci/home.asp.

The Compliance Institute, based in the UK, deals with compliance activities in the financial services industry and publishes *The Gazette*. The Compliance Institute, 107 Barkby Road, Leicester LE4 9LG, UK. Phone (in the UK) is (0)116 2461316. Email is: hlacey.compinst@btconnect.com. Its Website is http://www.complianceinstitute.co.uk.

The Defense Industry Initiative on Business Ethics and Conduct (DII) "is a consortium of U.S. defense industry contractors which subscribes to a set of principles for achieving high standards of business ethics and conduct." It can be contacted through Richard J. Bednar, Senior Counsel, Crowell & Moring LLP, 1001 Pennsylvania Avenue, N.W. Suite 1000 Washington D.C. 20004-2595, Telephone: 202-624-2619. Its Web address is www.dii.org/.

Ethics and Compliance and Custodian Organization, in South Africa, has among its goals providing support for managers with ethics and compliance responsibilities through research, training and benchmark standards. Its Web address is http://www.ethics.up.ac.za/goals.html.

Ethics and Compliance Officer Association, Keith Darcy, Executive Director (617-484-9400), Website www.theecoa.org. This organization is open to those who are in-house conducting compliance/ethics work.

Health Care Compliance Association, Roy Snell. Phone 888-580-8373. Membership is open to anyone interested in compliance/ethics in the health care field. Information on positions in the field is provided at www.hcca-info.org/Content/NavigationMenu/Compliance_Resources/Career_Opportunities/Career_Opportunities.htm.

International Association of Privacy Professionals, 266 York Street, York, Maine 03909, Phone 207-351-1500 or 800-266-6501. Its Website is www. privacyassociation.org. The site includes employment positions in the privacy compliance field.

The International Compliance Association is a UK-based non-profit professional organization dedicated to the furtherance of best compliance and anti money laundering practice in the financial services sector. Its Web address is www.int-comp.org.

The International Ombudsman Association, formerly the Ombudsman Association, 203 Towne Centre Drive, Hillsborough, NJ 08844-4693. Its Website is http://www.ombudsassociation.org/.

The National Society of Compliance Professionals is a non-profit membership organization for compliance professionals in the securities industry. 22 Kent Road, Cornwall Bridge, CT 06754, Tel: (860) 672-0843, Email: info@nscp.org. Its Website is http://www.nscp.org/.

Society of Corporate Compliance & Ethics, 6500 Barrie Road, Suite 250, Minneapolis, MN 55435, Tel: (888) 277-4977; email info@ corporatecompliance.org, Website www.corporatecompliance.org. An international, non-profit organization dedicated to improving the quality of corporate governance, compliance and ethics.

Resources on the subject of Compliance/Business Ethics:

Ad Hoc Advisory Group on the Organizational Sentencing Guidelines, *Report* (Oct. 7, 2003), http://www.ussc.gov/corp/advgrprpt/advgrprpt.htm.

BNA/ACCA, Compliance Manual, two-volume updated book on corporate compliance. (800) 372-1033.

Compliance & Ethics, published bi-monthly by the Society of Corporate Compliance and Ethics (888) 277-4977. Offers peer review articles on issues that compliance and ethics professionals grapple with each day.

Compliance Week, weekly publication addressing corporate compliance and governance for US public companies. (888) 519-9200 info@ complianceweek.com.

Crawford, D. B., C. Chaffin and S. Scarborough, *Effective Compliance Systems: A Practical Guide for Educational Institutions,* (Altamonte Springs, Fla.: The Institute of Internal Auditors Research Foundation, 2001).

ethikos, published bi-monthly, (914) 381-7475. Reports on practical approaches to compliance and ethics. Its Website is http://www.singerpubs.com/ethikos/

Kaplan, Jeffrey M., Joseph E. Murphy and Winthrop M. Swenson, *Compliance Programs and the Corporate Sentencing Guidelines* (Eagan, Minn.: Thompson/West Publishers; 1993 & annual supplement).

Murphy, Joseph E., *Compliance Primer: A Guide to the World of Corporate Ethics and Compliance Programs.* This is a primer on compliance and ethics, including a chronology of the field and an explanation of the basics. It is available from Integrity Interactive Corporation, (781) 891-9700, www.integrity-interactive.com.

Prevention of Corporate Liability Current Report, BNA's monthly news report on corporate compliance. (800) 372-1033.

U.S. Sentencing Commission, organizational sentencing guidelines, www.ussc.gov/orgguide.htm.

Appendix D

Compliance: War Story Reading

One of the best ways to learn a subject is from real-life experiences. The field of corporate crime and misconduct is, unfortunately, filled with examples. Here are some of the war stories that can introduce you to the world of corporate misconduct and give you a feel for why compliance programs have become so important and why the compliance job can call for the best you can give it.

1. Braithwaite, John, *Corporate Crime in the Pharmaceutical Industry* (London: Routledge & Kegan Paul Books Ltd.,1984)—This is not one story, but a review of an entire industry. Although it is primarily historical now, the lessons are still important.

2. Bruck, Connie, *The Predators' Ball: The Inside Story of Drexel Burnham and the Rise of the Junk Bond Raiders* (New York: Penguin Books, 1989)—The junk bond era and the days of Drexel Burnham.

3. Byrne, John A., *Informed Consent* (New York: McGraw-Hill Companies, 1996)—A story about the Dow Corning breast implant controversy, told generally from the perspective of a company ethics officer.

4. Carpenter, Donna Sammons & John Feloni, *The Fall of the House of Hutton* (New York: HarperCollins, 1989)—Almost forgotten after Drexel and Enron, this was a shocking debacle at a once-respected brokerage house.

5. Driscoll, Dawn-Marie, W. Michael Hoffman & Edward Petry, *The Ethical Edge: Tales of Organizations That Have Faced Moral Crises* (Darby, Penn.: Diane Books Publishing Company, 1995)—A useful collection of war stories from companies that have gotten in trouble.

6. Eichenwald, Kurt, *Conspiracy of Fools* (New York: Broadway Books, 2005)—Another rendition of the Enron debacle, told by one of the great, in-depth corporate crime reporters.

7. Eichenwald, Kurt, *The Informant* (New York: Broadway books, 2000)—One of the strangest stories in the business crime field—Mark Whitacre and the ADM price-fixing case.

8. Eichenwald, Kurt, *Serpent on the Rock* (New York: Broadway Books, 2005)—The story of scandal at Pru-Bache, by a New York Times reporter who covered the story.

9. Frantz, Douglas, *Levine and Company: Wall Street's Insider Trading Scandal* (New York: Avon Books, 1987)—The story of Dennis Levine, the first major shoe to drop, leading to the unraveling of the Wall Street scandal featuring the likes of Boesky and Milken.

10. Jeter, Lynne W., *Disconnected: Deceit and Betrayal at WorldCom* (New York: John Wiley & Sons, 2004)—Tells the tale of one of the most dramatic stories in the "Enron Era"—the collapse of WorldCom.

11. McLean, Bethany & Peter Elkind, *The Smartest Guys in the Room: The Amazing Rise and Scandalous Fall of Enron* (New York: Portfolio Books, 2003)—The best told story about Enron. Strong on detail, plus an interesting read.

12. Mokhiber, Russell, *Corporate Crime and Violence: Big Business Power and the Abuse of the Public Trust* (New York: Random House, Inc., 1988). Not for the faint of heart, this book, written from a Naderite perspective, inventories major corporate compliance debacles and the harm that they caused.

13. Pasztor, Andy, *When the Pentagon Was for Sale: Inside America's Biggest Defense Scandal* (New York: Scribner, 1995)—The story of "Ill Wind," the massive defense scandal that was the basis for creation of the Defense Industry Initiative, one of the first major compliance-oriented industry groups.

14. Pollock, Ellen, *The Pretender: How Martin Frankel Fooled the Financial World and Led the Feds on One of the Most Publicized Manhunts in History* (New York: Free Press, 2002)—A remarkable illustration of how even an unlikely offender can fool people who should have known better.

15. Roberts, Bari-Ellen & Jack E. White, *Roberts vs. Texaco* (New York: Harper Perennial,1999)—An insider's story of discrimination inside a major corporation.

16. Smith, Rebecca & John R. Emshwiller, *24 Days* (New York: HarperCollins, 2003)—Recounts the Enron story from the perspective of two Wall Street Journal reporters who initially broke the story.

17. Stewart, James B., *Den of Thieves* (New York: Simon & Schuster, 1991)—Back to the days of the junk bond king, hostile takeovers and the fall of Drexel Burnham.

18. Swartz, Mimi, with Sherron Watkins, *Power Failure: The Inside Story of the Collapse of Enron* (New York: Doubleday, 2003)—Insights from Enron's in-house whistleblower, Sherron Watkins. Provides a "you were there" feel.

19. Toffler, Barbara Ley & Jennifer Reingold, *Final Accounting: Ambition, Greed and the Fall of Arthur Andersen* (New York: Currency Books, 2003)—An insider's view of what happened at Andersen. There is a special irony here—the author worked for Andersen selling compliance services to customers, but could not get Andersen to adopt a compliance program.

Appendix E

Ethics Centers

What are Ethics Centers?

As you look into a possible career in compliance and ethics, you will undoubtedly come across a slew of ethics centers. What exactly are they, and how can they help you develop your career in this field? In this appendix, we briefly look at ethics centers, and provide a list of centers.

Ethics Centers come in a variety of shapes and sizes, with names as varied as their foci. While most share the "center" (or "centre") designation, often that is where the similarity ends. Some few "centers" you encounter will in fact be primarily consulting businesses, and should be approached as such; most however will not be. Frequently attached to or funded by an academic institution, ethics centers exist to research, teach or otherwise promote the discussion of ethics topics among members of their target audience, which is more often students and faculty than the general public. Occasionally, an academic program or department will be known as a "Center."

Centers focus on a variety of ethics areas, including Business Ethics, Applied Ethics, Bioethics, Corporate Social Responsibility, Environmental Regulation, Ethics in the Workplace, and Applied Religious Ethics. Centers usually have a small staff with perhaps one or two paid employees (a director and coordinator or secretary). Some centers of note have subject matter experts on their advisory boards, guiding research or overseeing center events, but most centers will depend on volunteers for additional staff. Sometimes centers have an assigned room or building, and sometimes they exist solely online or in a faculty lounge or employee office. Availability of resources and staff will limit specific activities, but many centers offer small publications, organize discussions, or bring in expert speakers in the area of their focus. These events will again likely be limited to members of associated organizations, though some will be open to the public.

What is their value?

As varied in focus and resources as these centers are, their specific value from a compliance and ethics career perspective may be hard to determine. In general, you will not find many opportunities for a paying job within an ethics center, excepting when you work with an affiliated organization or have some other connection that may lead the center to invite you onto their staff. In our research, few centers we encountered have the resources to hire someone "off the street." For those non-academic centers that are in the consulting business, the approach for these is covered in the chapter on getting into the field (Chapter 3).

What else can an ethics center do for you? As you apply for jobs elsewhere in compliance, or perhaps before that, when you are still trying to figure out what this field is about, ethics centers may be a good source for training, networking, reading materials, or online Web resources. The most important step in acquiring these resources is to determine the focus of a particular ethics center. This can usually be accomplished via a Website or a single quick call/email. If a Website exists, we advise visiting it first. When the center's focus is in line with your interests, you can then pursue their resources safely without fear of completely wasting your time (knowledge of environmental regulation turmoil will hardly help the aspiring online data privacy professional).

What is the harm in looking? Is it worth it?

Centers are often limited in focus, and if that focus does not include applied ethics, you should move right along. Philosophical ethics is intellectually stimulating, but it is usually not going to pay the bills. To quote the movie *Dragon: The Bruce Lee Story*, a degree in philosophy allows you to "think deep thoughts about being unemployed." (Note: one of the authors happily minored in philosophy.) But not only can an irrelevant focus slow you down, but so too will you discover many ethics centers simply are not able to help you. Many offer their services only to those students and members of associated organizations, and if you are not associated, you are not invited.

These centers usually have limited budgets and staff, and if their mission is to elucidate students/employees or train teachers, they simply do not have the scope or resources to help you. Very few centers currently provide significant certification or training of any kind to the public. For this kind of service, you will likely need to seek out a membership organization or company that specializes in those offerings. We have included this information in Chapter 9, "What Training and Certifications are Available for Compliance Professionals?"

When a center is willing to offer help, and most staff members at centers are friendly enough when contacted, keep in mind their availability. Part-time staff or staff with other responsibilities may not be reached easily. So too may staff rotate out, or even disappear entirely between phone calls or emails if the center reaches the end of its budgeted existence (many are funded by one-time grants, or are budgeted only for a year or semester). So if you are going to contact ethics centers, act fast. An exciting resource here today may be gone tomorrow.

And these centers may be just that for you personally: an exciting resource. If you need information on a certain topic for a project or publication, there may be an ethics center out there just for you. Many centers offer extensive Web links and publications on their focus topic, so when you can find them, book-mark or print to your heart's desire. But unless you specifically hear about a center that suits your needs, we do not advise devoting much time to the search, from a career-development standpoint. You will find Websites for a great many centers, many with multiple pages and resource lists, much of which might be out-of-date.

To provide you with a basic guide to the ethics center terrain, here is some preliminary information about ethics centers.

Ethics Centers

Centers are listed alphabetically, and listings include location/affiliations, a brief focus/mission assessment, Web address, telephone number, and primary email contact, when each is available.

Note that our assessment of focus may not include all goals of the center. Our choices were based on the prominent points on the centers' Web pages.

1. **The Association for Practical and Professional Ethics**
   Location: Indiana University
   Focus: Interdisciplinary scholarship, teaching in practical & professional ethics, environmental, business, medical, legal, communications, military
   Website: http://www.indiana.edu/~appe/
   Phone: (812) 855-6450
   Email: appe@indiana.edu (questions pertaining to the Website)

2. **The Bauer Center for Business Ethics**
   Location: University of Houston
   Focus: Introducing students to business ethics requires a capstone course; encourages faculty to cover ethics
   Website: http://www.bauer.uh.edu/BCBE/
   Phone: (713) 743-4600 (C. T. Bauer College of Business, Univ. of Houston)

3. **The Berg Center for Ethics and Leadership**
   Location: University of Pittsburgh
   Focus: Explore link between ethics and leadership accomplished through research, education and sponsored activities
   Website: http://www.pitt.edu/~bergcntr/index.htm
   Phone: (412) 648-2169 (Erin Seifert, Coordinator)
   Email: bergcenter@katz.pitt.edu

4. **The Carol and Lawrence Zicklin Center for Business Ethics Research**
   Location: University of Pennsylvania
   Focus: Research in business ethics topics, global business ethics, corporate governance, social contracts
   Website: http://www.zicklincenter.org/
   Phone: (215) 898-1166
   Email: tomascol@wharton.upenn.edu (Lauretta Tomasco, Associate Director)

5. **The Center for Applied Christian Ethics (CACE)**
   Location: Wheaton College
   Focus: Application of biblical ethics to contemporary moral decisions; events include debates and conferences; offers other resources
   Website: www.christianethics.org
   Phone: (630) 752-5886
   Email: cace@wheaton.edu

6. **The Center for Applied and Professional Ethics (CAPE)**
   Location: California State University
   Focus: Promotes ethical reflection inside and outside of the university; sponsors public lectures and discussions; assists teaching and research, etc.
   Website: http://www.csuchico.edu/cape/
   Phone: (530) 898-5534 (Andrew Flescher, Ph.D., Director, Cape)
   Email: aflescher@csuchico.edu
   (Andrew Flescher, Ph.D., Director, Cape)

7. **The Center for Applied and Professional Ethics (CAPE)**
   Location: University of Tennessee
   Focus: Facilitate discussion of practical and applied ethics; works with both those inside the university and in neighboring areas
   Website: http://web.utk.edu/~philosop/cape.html
   Phone: (865) 974-3255
   Email: jhardwig@utk.edu (John Hardwig, CAPE Director)

8. **The Center for Business Ethics**
   Location: Bentley College
   Focus: Align effective business performance with ethical business conduct; offering leadership; lectures, scholarships, programs like MEO
   Website: http://ecampus.bentley.edu/dept/cbe/
   Phone: (781) 891-2981
   Email: cbeinfo@bentley.edu

9. **Center for Business Ethics and Social Responsibility**

   Location: Xavier University

   Focus: Act as resource to students, faculty, and local and national business; offers continuing education program and web site resources.

   Website: http://www.xavier.edu/business_ethics/

   Phone: (513) 745-2050 (Paul Fiorelli, Director)

   Email: fiorelli@xavier.edu (Paul Fiorelli, Director)

10. **The Center for Ethics**

    Location: Emory University

    Focus: Spreading ethics knowledge and practice; offers an Ethics Minor, seminars, etc.

    Website: http://www.ethics.emory.edu/

    Phone: (404) 727-4954

11. **The Center for Ethics**

    Location: University of Montana-Missoula

    Focus: Promote teaching, research, service in applied and professional ethics; will tailor grad Ph.D.; offers short summer courses in ethics for credit or learning

    Website: http://www.umt.edu/ethics/

    Phone: (406) 243-5744

    Email: ethics@mso.umt.edu

12. **Center for Ethics**

    Location: University of Tampa

    Focus: Promote ethics, responsibility in academics and business; research; numerous programs, including an annual breakfast, award.

    Website: http://www.ut.edu/institutes/cobcenters/cfe/

13. **The Center for Ethics and Business**

    Location: Loyola Marymount University

    Focus: Fosters discussions on difficulty, costs, rewards, etc., of ethical business; holds an annual two-week event; offers web site resources, etc.

    Website: http://www.ethicsandbusiness.org

    Email: jgoodkind@lmu.edu

14. **The Center for Ethics and Humanities in the Life Sciences**
    Location: Michigan State University
    Focus: Bring ethics and humanities thought to health care and science; an educational resource via teaching, writing, speaking, research, etc.
    Website: http://www.bioethics.msu.edu/
    Phone: (517) 355-7550
    Email: center@msu.edu

15. **The Center for Ethics and Human Rights**
    Location: American Nurses Association
    Focus: Addresses ethical and human rights issues faced by nurses; offers consultation and participates in committees
    Website: http://www.nursingworld.org/ethics/
    Phone: (301) 628-5000
    Email: ethics@ana.org

16. **Center for Ethics and Public Service**
    Location: University of Miami
    Focus: Clinical program, ethical judgement, responsibility and public service; works via clinics and educational programs
    Website: http://www.law.miami.edu/ceps/index.html
    Phone: (305) 284-3934
    Email: jumunoz@law.miami.edu (Julia Muñoz, Senior Staff Assistant)

17. **The Center for Ethics and Social Justice**
    Location: Loyola University Chicago
    Focus: Provides ethics education, inside and outside university; workshops, conferences, adviceline for journalists
    Website: http://www.luc.edu/ethics/
    Phone: (773) 508-8349
    Email: ethics@luc.edu

18. **The Center for Professional and Applied Ethics**
    Location: University of North Carolina at Charlotte
    Focus: Grow moral awareness, ethics skills of faculty, students, professionals; courses, graduate certificate program, speakers, publications, etc.
    Website: http://www.uncc.edu/ethics/
    Phone: (704) 687-2850
    Email: rotong@email.uncc.edu (Rosemarie Tong, Director)

19. **The Center for Professional Ethics**
Location: Case Western Reserve University
Focus: Aid students, faculty, professionals w/ personal and professional ethics; offers a newsletter, etc.
Website: http://www.case.edu/groups/cpe/cpe.html
Phone: (216) 368-5349

20. **The Center for Professional Values and Practice**
Location: New York Law School
Focus: Examines roles of lawyers and norms and values guiding their conduct; curriculum, symposia, various initiatives, etc.
Website: http://www.nyls.edu/pages/502.asp
Phone: (212) 431-2314
Email: ckendall@nyls.edu (Chris Alan Kendall, Program Director)

21. **Center for Religion, Ethics and Social Policy (CRESP)**
Location: Cornell University
Focus: Help build a just and sustainable society; works through campus and neighboring areas in various projects
Website: http://www.cresp.cornell.edu/index.php
Phone: (607) 255-5027 (Anke Wessels, Ph.D., Director)
Email: akw7@cornell.edu (Anke Wessels, Ph.D., Director)

22. **The Center for the Study of Ethics**
Location: Utah Valley State College
Focus: Promote study of ethics in students, faculty and community; works through curriculum, forums, workshops and publications
Website: http://www.uvsc.edu/ethics/
Phone: (801) 863-8455
Email: ethics.center@uvsc.edu

23. **The Center for the Study of Ethics in the Professions (CSEP)**
Location: Illinois Institute of Technology
Focus: Promote education and scholarship concerning the professions; publications, ethics bowl, online codes of ethics section, workshop
Website: http://ethics.iit.edu/
Phone: (312) 567-3017
Email: csep@iit.edu

24. **Center for the Study of Ethics in Society**

    Location: Western Michigan University

    Focus: Service to community and university in applied and professional ethics; research, teaching, publications, etc.

    Website: http://www.wmich.edu/ethics/

    Phone: (269) 387-4397

    Email: ethicscenter@wmich.edu

25. **The Edmond J. Safra Foundation Center for Ethics**

    Location: Harvard University

    Focus: Teaching/research on ethical issues in public and professional life; moral choice in business, education, government, etc.; varied resources

    Website: http://www.ethics.harvard.edu/

    Phone: (617) 495-1336

    Email: ethics@harvard.edu

26. **The Ethics Institute**

    Location: Dartmouth College

    Focus: Foster study of applied and professional ethics at Dartmouth; offers many programs, including courses, discussions

    Website: http://www.dartmouth.edu/~ethics/

    Phone: (603) 646-1263

    Email: Ethics.Institute@Dartmouth.EDU

27. **The Ethics and Public Policy Center (EPPC)**

    Location: Washington, D.C.

    Focus: Judeo-Christian morals and domestic, foreign policy issues; works through various conferences, programs and publications

    Website: http://www.eppc.org/

    Phone: (202) 682-1200

    Email: Ethics@eppc.org.

28. **The Ethics Resource Center**

    Location: Washington, D.C.

    Focus: Strengthen ethical leadership worldwide; organizational ethics; assessing compliance programs; white papers

    Website: www.ethics.org

    Phone: (202) 737-2258

    Email: ethics@ethics.org

29. **Gonzaga Ethics Institute**
Location: Gonzaga University
Focus: Provide ethics resources and programs to Gonzaga, neighboring areas; offers the Ethics Advantage Program, workshops, and other programs
Website: http://www.gonzaga.edu/Campus+Resources/Offices+ and+Services+A-Z/Gonzaga+Ethics+Institute/default.asp
Phone: (509) 323-5519
Email: stebbins@gonzaga.edu (J. Michael Stebbins, Ph.D, Director)

30. **The Hastings Center**
Location: Garrison, NY
Focus: Research in health care, biotechnology and environment; conducts research and puts out several publications
Website: http://www.thehastingscenter.org/
Phone: (845) 424-4040
Email: mail@thehastingscenter.org

31. **The Hoffberger Center for Professional Ethics**
Location: University of Baltimore
Focus: Promote awareness and discussion of ethics at the university; provides faculty, internships and public programs
Website: http://www.ubalt.edu/hoffberger/
Phone: (410) 837-5379
Email: hoffberger@ubalt.edu

32. **The Institute for Applied & Professional Ethics**
Location: Ohio University
Focus: Promote ethical decisions; workshops, conferences, supports grad students and faculty
Website: http://freud.citl.ohiou.edu/ethics/index.php
Phone: (740) 593-9802
Email: ethics@ohio.edu

33. **The Institute for Business & Professional Ethics (IBPE)**
Location: DePaul University
Focus: Encourage ethical deliberation in Chicago organizations and at Depaul; annual conference, academic programs, subject matter experts
Website: http://commerce.depaul.edu/ethics/
Phone: (312) 362-8793 (Dr. Patricia Werhane, Executive Director)
Email: pwerhane@depaul.edu (Dr. Patricia Werhane, Executive Director)

34. **The Interfaith Center on Corporate Responsibility (ICCR)**
    Location: New York, NY
    Focus: Leading in corporate social responsibility movement; publications; members factor social values into investments
    Website: http://www.iccr.org/
    Phone: (212) 870-2295
    Email: info@iccr.org

35. **Institute for Global Ethics**
    Location: Camden, ME
    Focus: Promoting ethical behavior through research, discourse and action; provide services to strengthen ethics in organizations, etc.
    Website: http://www.globalethics.org/index.htm
    Phone: (207) 236-6658; (800) 729-2615
    Email: ethics@globalethics.org

36. **The International Center for Ethics, Justice and Public Life**
    Location: Brandeis University
    Focus: Respond to conflict and injustice through ethical practice; lectures, courses, publications, seminars, etc.
    Website: http://www.brandeis.edu/ethics/about/index.html
    Phone: (781) 736-8577
    Email: ethics@brandeis.edu

37. **Investor Responsibility Research Center**
    Location: Washington, D.C.
    Focus: Provide impartial information on governance and social responsibility; this company provides various products, services and publications
    Website: http://www.irrc.com
    Phone: (202) 833-0700
    Email: marketing@irrc.com

38. **Joan and David Lincoln Center for Applied Ethics**
    Location: Arizona State University
    Focus: Create an ethical culture in the university and community; offers Award for Public Virtue, conferences, courses
    Website: http://www.asu.edu/clas/lincolncenter/
    Phone: (480) 727-7691
    Email: LincolnCenter@asu.edu

39. **Joseph & Edna Josephson Institute of Ethics**
Location: Los Angeles, CA
Focus: Improve society's ethical culture by changing decision-making; offers various programs and workshops, a training seminar
Website: http://www.josephsoninstitute.org/
Phone: (310) 846-4800

40. **The Joseph P. and Rose F. Kennedy Institute of Ethics**
Location: Georgetown University
Focus: Serve as an ethics resource for research, study, debate, policy makers; offers publications, courses, programs, and an online library
Website: http://kennedyinstitute.georgetown.edu/
Phone: (202) 687-8099

41. **The Kegley Institute of Ethics**
Location: Bakersfield, CA
Focus: Encourage involvement in ethical issues; act as an ethics resource; lectures, scholarships, publications, etc.
Website: http://www.csubak.edu/kie/IO.htx
Phone: (661) 664-3149 (Christopher Meyers, Ph.D., Executive Director)
Email: cmeyers@csub.edu (Christopher Meyers, Ph.D., Executive Director)

42. **The Kenan Institute for Ethics**
Location: Duke University
Focus: Support study/teaching of ethics, moral reflection & commitment in life; offers numerous programs, conferences, lectures, grants/awards, etc.
Website: http://kenan.ethics.duke.edu/
Phone: (919) 660-3033
Email: kie@duke.edu

43. **The Louis Stein Center for Law & Ethics**
Location: Fordham University
Focus: Promoting integration of ethics in legal practice; offers many conferences and publications
Website: http://law.fordham.edu/htm/st-home.htm

44. **The Markkula Center for Applied Ethics**

Location: Santa Clara University

Focus: Resource for those wishing to apply an ethical approach to world issues; ethics areas include business, global, government, technology, etc.

Website: http://www.scu.edu/ethics/

Phone: (408) 554-5319

Email: ethics@scu.edu

45. **Olsson Center for Applied Ethics**

Location: University of Virginia

Focus: Resource for integrating ethics into business decision-making; lectures, publications, research projects, teaching

Website: http://www.darden.virginia.edu/olsson

Phone: (434) 924-7247

Email: ref8d@virginia.edu

46. **The Poynter Center for the Study of Ethics and American Institutions**

Location: Indiana University Bloomington

Focus: Studying ethical issues and initiating research and teaching; offers public seminars, workshops and lectures; publications

Website: http://www.indiana.edu/~poynter/

Phone: (812) 855-0261

Email: poynter@indiana.edu

47. **The University Center for Human Values**

Location: Princeton University

Focus: Promote research, teaching, discussion of ethics and values at Princeton; offers programs, publications, videos, etc.

Website: http://www.princeton.edu/values/

Centers Outside of the United States

48. **Centre for Applied Ethics (CAE)**

Location: Hong Kong Baptist University (Hong Kong)

Focus: Promote thought about ethics concerns & moral values; lectures; research projects; assisting organizations with ethics courses

Website: http://cae.hkbu.edu.hk/

Phone: (852)-3411-7274

Email: cae@hkbu.edu.hk

49. **Centre for Applied Philosophy and Public Ethics (CAPPE)**
   Location: The Australian National University (Australia)
   Focus: Research and promote discussion on public and political concerns; workshops, conferences, consultancy, graduate training, etc.
   Website: http://www.cappe.edu.au/
   Phone: +61 2 61258467
   Email: cappe@csu.edu.au

50. **Centre for Professional and Applied Ethics**
   Location: University of Manitoba (Canada)
   Focus: Encourage research, scholarly activity in professional & applied ethics; offers fellowships, publications, consultation, lectures, etc.
   Website: http://www.umanitoba.ca/centres/ethics/
   Phone: (204) 474-9107
   Email: ethics@cc.umanitoba.ca

51. **The Unilever Ethics Centre**
   Location: University of Natal (South Africa)
   Focus: Provide ethics knowledge, skills, methods, and other resources; offers courses, seminars, workshops; consultancy, research, etc.
   Website: http://www.ethics.ukzn.ac.za/centre.htm
   Phone: +27 (0)33 260 5573
   Email: ethics@ukzn.ac.za

52. **W. Maurice Young Centre for Applied Ethics (CAE)**
   Location: The University of British Columbia (Vancouver, B.C.)
   Focus: Advance research in applied ethics, offer courses, and act as a resource; research projects, graduate education, ethics training, consulting, etc.
   Website: http://www.ethics.ubc.ca/
   Phone: (604) 822-8625
   Email: plewis@ethics.ubc.ca (Patrick Lewis, Research Manager)

This appendix was formed based on a survey performed by one of the authors, Joshua Leet, working with Christopher Vigale, a former Compliance Analyst with Compliance Systems Legal Group. The authors would like to thank the following individuals for taking the time to speak with us.

- Erin Seifert, Coordinator, Berg Center
- Lauretta Tomasco, Associate Director, Zicklin Center
- Dr. Kenneth Chase, Director, Center for Applied Christian Ethics
- Paul Fiorelli, Director, Center for Business Ethics and Social Responsibility

- Thomas I. White, Ph.D., Director, Center for Ethics and Business
- Robert Lawry, Director, Center for Professional Ethics)
- Chris Alan Kendall, Director, Center for Professional Values and Practice
- Joyce Raskin, Project Director, Stein Center
- Jim Balassone, Executive in Residence, Markkula Center

Appendix F

There Is More...

As described in the Preface, this book is actually an abridged version of a longer book, *Working for Integrity: Finding the Perfect Job in the Rapidly Growing Compliance and Ethics Field*. The larger book contains substantially more information, including more than 20 interviews, several additional chapters and chapter appendices, and increased depth in every other chapter. Topics addressed include the pitfalls or dangers of this work, protections from those dangers, how to move into the field from another job, and how to hire from the company's point of view. Expanded sections in chapters you have seen include the job title appendix from chapter 4 of this book (which contains more than 800 titles) and the selling Tips from chapter 10 of this book (which contains 4 additional tips).

If you are serious about starting a career in this field, or enhancing the one you already have, this other book will be a great resource to you.

On the next page, we have included the full Table of Contents from that book, where you can see each major topic that we cover in the larger book.

Following the Table of Contents, we have provided information on ordering your own copy of *Working for Integrity: Finding the Perfect Job in the Rapidly Growing Compliance and Ethics Field*.

Working for Integrity: Finding the Perfect Job in the Rapidly Growing Compliance and Ethics Field
Table of Contents
Foreword: Why This Book?
1. What Is This Field?
2. Why Should I Go into This Field?
   Appendix 2A "Should I Go into Compliance and Ethics? Some Questions to Ask Yourself."
3. How Do I Get into This Field?
   Appendix 3A "Resume Builders: Things You Can Do to Advance in the Compliance and Ethics Field."
4. What Are the Jobs in This Field?
   Appendix 4A "What's in a Name? Titles and Positions in the Compliance and Ethics Field"
   4B "Compliance Officer Position Description"
   4C "Assistant Compliance Officer Position Description"

To order *Working for Integrity: Finding the Perfect Job in the Rapidly Growing Compliance and Ethics Field*, visit the Website of the Society of Corporate Compliance and Ethics (SCCE) at www.corporatecompliance.org. Navigate to the store and into the books section. Or you may order a copy directly by mailing in the order form on the following page.

For more information on the books and the project, visit the authors' blog at workingforintegrity.blogspot.com/. There you will find information about special appearances by the authors promoting the book, update information, plans for future projects, articles relating to the books, interview excerpts and additional information relating to working in compliance and ethics. You may also send the authors information, resources, and suggestions through the blog.

For information about joining the Society of Corporate Compliance & Ethics, see www.corporatecompliance.org.

ORDER FORM

Working for Integrity: Finding the Perfect Job in the Rapidly Growing Compliance and Ethics Field

❑ *Working for Integrity* (SCCE Member Price) $145.00

❑ *Working for Integrity* (Non-Member Price) $195.00

(Free FedEx Ground shipping within continental U.S.)

Please type or print:

_____
SCCE Member ID

_____
First Name   M.I.   Last Name

_____
Title

_____
Organization

_____
Street Address

_____
City   State   Zip

_____
Telephone

_____
Fax

_____
Email

Please make your check payable to SCCE. For more information, call +1 952 933 4977 or 888 277 4977.

Mail check to: 6500 Barrie Road, Suite 250, Minneapolis, MN 55435, USA | **Or fax to:** +1 952 988 0146

Total: $ _____

❑ Check enclosed

❑ Invoice me   ❑ PO # _____

Charge my credit card: ❑ Mastercard ❑ VISA ❑ American Express

_____
Account number

_____
Expiration date

_____
Name on card

_____
Signature

Federal Tax ID: 23-2882664. Prices subject to change without notice. SCCE is required to charge sales tax on purchases from Minnesota and Pennsylvania. Please calculate this in the cost of your order. The required sales tax in Pennsylvania is 7% and Minnesota is 6.9%.

SOCIETY OF CORPORATE
COMPLIANCE AND ETHICS

6500 Barrie Road, Suite 250, Minneapolis, MN 55435, United States
Phone +1 952 933 4977 or 888 277 4977 | FAX +1 952 988 0146
helpteam@corporatecompliance.org | www.corporatecompliance.org